NOIR White Paper

PART ONE
True Psychology of the Insider Spy

PART TWO
Proposing a New Policy
For Improving National Security
By Fixing the Problem of Insider Spies

PART THREE
Prevention: The Missing Link
For Managing Insider Threat
in the Intelligence Community

*Counterintelligence Is the Stepchild
of The Intelligence Community*

Prevention Is the Stepchild of Counterintelligence

Detection Gets All the Love

Dr. David L. Charney
Psychiatrist

"I am utterly amazed to find this [paper] that accurately describes the true experiences of the spy. Reading the stages [of a spy] actually made me tremble as I recalled my own entry into the world of espionage and the inevitable consequences."

–Jens Karney (aka Jeffrey M. Carney)
former US Air Force Intelligence Specialist and spy for the GDR's Ministry of State Security (MfS)

TABLE OF CONTENTS

PART ONE
TRUE PSYCHOLOGY OF THE INSIDER SPY

THE PROBLEM OF INSIDER SPIES has bedeviled intelligence services from time immemorial. Over the years, government intelligence agencies have made significant efforts to preemptively screen out prospective traitors. Nevertheless, all the world's intelligence services have suffered penetrations, including our own.

Increasingly stringent security practices, such as more frequent follow-up background investigations, have been used to lessen the threat of insider spies. Americans have particularly favored advanced technology solutions. Nevertheless, these heroic measures seem to fail time and again. Strongly motivated spies have demonstrated the capacity to successfully discern the seams between the most well-thought-out protective measures – and have insidiously slipped through.

The intelligence community is no different from other domains in this respect. Firms in the private sector, such as Microsoft, have tried to protect their products from the depredations of hackers, but despite their enormous resources seem to be fighting a losing war. This reminds us that attention needs to be mainly focused on the workings of the mind of the insider spy.

And yet the mind of the insider spy remains obscure. While many studies have focused on trying to understand what makes the mind of the insider spy tick, progress in this understanding has been slow, and making good use of it has not been particularly successful. Efforts at predicting who will turn traitor have turned out to be mostly blind alleys.

The dirty little secret of spy detection has been that, almost always, insider spies have been revealed only when someone from the "other side" comes across bearing gifts of information to prove their *bona fides*.

If we were able to develop an improved understanding of insider spy psychology, we would have better chances of devising countermeasures that could succeed. This would represent just good intelligence practice applied to an issue critical to the intelligence community itself.

My work has permitted me to advance further towards what I call the true psychology of the insider spy. A decade of consulting as a clinical psychiatrist to some of our intelligence agencies and treating employees from all corners of the intelligence community, provided my initial immersion in the world of intelligence.

Then I was fortunate to be engaged as a consultant to the defense of three captured insider spies, including the notorious Robert Hanssen. While at first I had mixed feelings about joining their defense teams, I regarded involvement in these cases as unique opportunities that would enable me to understand the inner workings of the minds of insider spies.

The three insider spies I extensively interviewed. (L-R) Earl Pitts (FBI); Robert Hanssen (FBI); Brian Regan (Air Force/NRO)

I received cooperation from all three spies because I was working for them on the defense side, and also because of my frequent access: I could visit each for up to two hours weekly over an entire year.

The primary basis of my findings derives from my unprecedented close-contact experiences with these three insider spies. In addition, I intensively studied most of the other cases of insider spying in the United States that occurred during the twentieth century and up through the present that were reported upon in open sources. I studied these additional cases from the vantage point of an experienced psychiatrist.

I also had the advantage of my familiarity with these kinds of cases based on my intensive exposure to the insider spies I met with personally. Psychological patterns became apparent to me that might have escaped notice by others not similarly trained or experienced. The ideas presented here spring from these combined sources. I will put forward here a new paradigm for better understanding the minds of insider spies.

For the purposes of this discussion, I will discuss the relevant issues from the perspective of an invented composite insider spy. This will permit clarification of key observations while at the same time avoiding problems related to confidentiality.

The new paradigm will incorporate three key idea clusters: the core psychology of the insider spy; the ten life stages of the insider spy; and the existential dilemmas of the insider spy.

Of course, the psychology proposed here does not encompass all insider spies without exception. For example, there are a number of insider spies who seem to hark back to the ideological spies of the thirties and forties, and there are still other anomalous cases that come to mind. Even taking into account these exceptional cases, I believe that probing into them more deeply would reveal layers that would roughly correspond to the ideas I will present here.

THE CORE PSYCHOLOGY OF THE INSIDER SPY

An intolerable sense of personal failure, as privately defined by that person.

While another observer might appraise the life of the person in question as having been a very tough story indeed – but still not that bad – the observer's appraisal does not count for anything. Only the opinion of the person in question matters. The only meaningful fact is whether the prospective insider spy feels like a failure to the point of it being intolerable for him. Even so, few in this group will decide to turn traitor. What turns out to be key is how this intolerable sense of personal failure gets managed. Almost always, this is a state of mind based on male psychology. Over 95% of insider spies

are males. Injuries to male pride and ego are at the root of most cases of insider spying. Further comments on gender differences will follow.

THE TEN LIFE STAGES OF THE INSIDER SPY

The idea of Life Stages takes a dynamic rather than a static view of what makes for insider spying. A dynamic, evolving view gets away from mainstream explanations that insider spies are born bad, or that a fixed personality type will predict for insider spying. Thus, the usual suspects of insider spy motivations, those based on greed, sociopathy, ideology, ego and arrogance, are held as less important than the unfolding of the movie of a person's life.

As the movie unfolds, things happen to the main character, some good and some bad. Drama gets added when adversities, stresses, challenges and disappointments pile up in excess. Some of these adverse developments are due to poor personal choices. Perhaps more of them are due to sheer bad luck. Will the main character manage to survive and triumph despite all the threats and pitfalls? Or will he stumble or fall?

Thus, I favor the argument: Insider spies are not born – they're made. What is crucial is what befalls them during the course and arc of their lives. We will consider each of the ten life stages of insider spies in turn. (Please refer to the accompanying chart, which maps Inner Tension alongside the Ten Life Stages).

STAGE ONE: THE SENSITIZING STAGE

Growing up is not easy for most of us. We all face less than optimal experiences along the way, such as a harsh or absent father, a critical or moody mother, mean siblings, academic troubles, health problems, and love relationships that end hurtfully. While these negative experiences may scar and sensitize us, they do not necessarily damage us forever or predict for certain later failure. In fact, they may plant an abiding drive for surmounting adversity, or an ambition to fix life's inequities and set the world right, or they may light a fire in the belly for proving that we are actually smart, competent, and successful – no matter what others may have thought of us.

If having gone through a tough childhood reliably ruined chances for later achievement in life, and also predicted a likely turn towards insider spying, perhaps the vast majority of the entire intelligence, law enforce-

Ten Life Stages of the Insider Spy

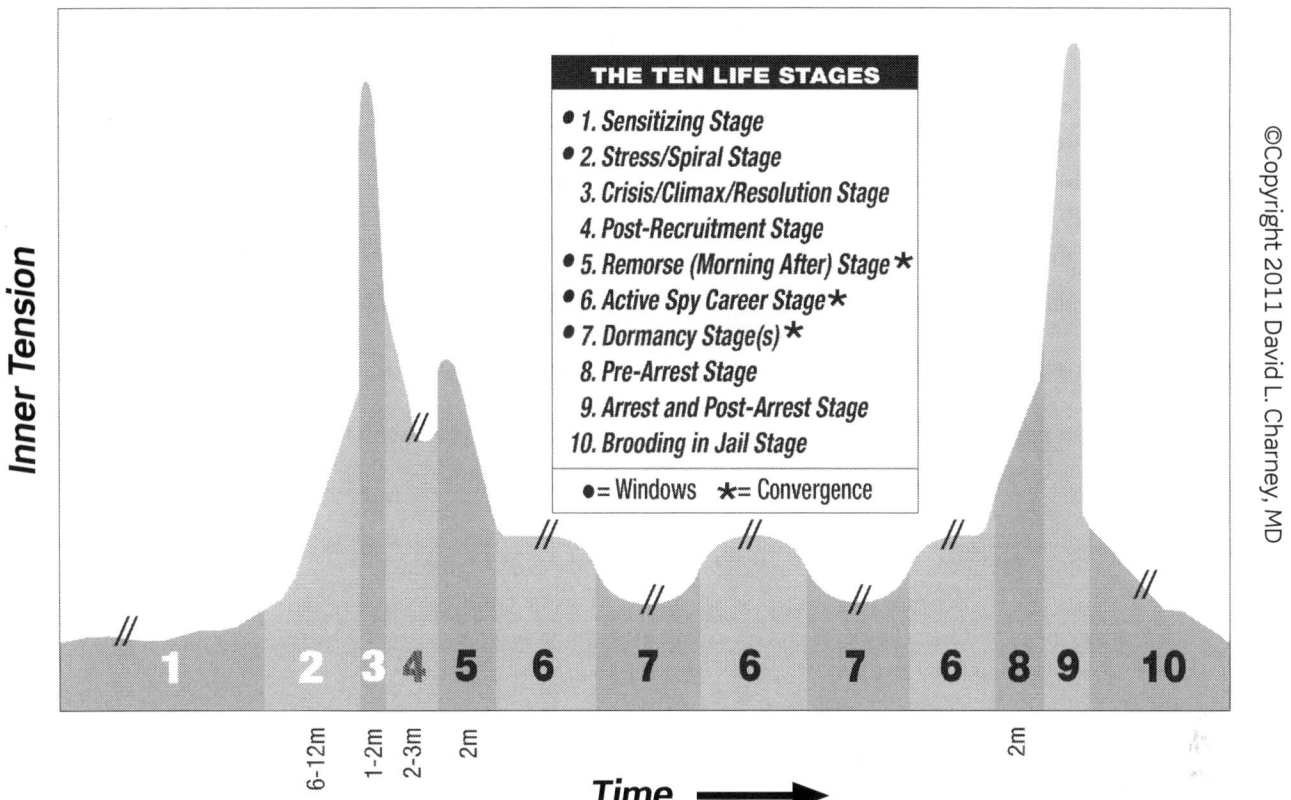

THE TEN LIFE STAGES

- 1. Sensitizing Stage
- 2. Stress/Spiral Stage
  3. Crisis/Climax/Resolution Stage
  4. Post-Recruitment Stage
- 5. Remorse (Morning After) Stage ★
- 6. Active Spy Career Stage ★
- 7. Dormancy Stage(s) ★
  8. Pre-Arrest Stage
  9. Arrest and Post-Arrest Stage
  10. Brooding in Jail Stage

● = Windows   ★ = Convergence

Inner Tension

Time ➡

ment and defense communities would have to be let go. Clearly, this makes no sense. While experiences can be truly hurtful and sensitizing, much more must happen later to tip the scales towards a decision to spy.

STAGE TWO: THE STRESS/SPIRAL STAGE

Entering the adult years brings more complex and demanding challenges. Now we tend to compare ourselves to others, while also facing up to our own expectations of ourselves. We all learn that natural gifts and talents alone do not result in sure success. Much of how it goes depends as much on external forces and blind luck. And for some unfortunates, the going can get very tough.

The bell-shaped curve of life is merciless. At one end of the curve, the good end, live the fortunate few for whom everything falls into place like ripe fruit, everything they touch turns to gold. At the other end – the bad end – just the opposite happens. Here live the unfortunate few for whom nothing goes right. Given a large enough population, say a government agency, it becomes a statistical likelihood that a small and very unlucky minority will experience the worst calamities of the bad end of the bell-shaped curve.

Adding further injury, the coincidental timing of life's hard knocks can really pile on, making it even worse, a situation I call a *Psychological Perfect Storm*. Even the strongest can waver in such a storm. We all like to think we could weather anything that comes our way. But try adding impending financial bankruptcy, severe personal health threats, an IRS audit, teenage son getting arrested, spouse having an affair, teenage daughter getting pregnant – all at the same time – and one can imagine even the strongest person buckling under the pressures. The Biblical story of Job addresses this awful possibility. What adds up to the breaking point for any individual will vary and is probably not predictable. Look for the key life setbacks that helped tip over to the decision to spy in the six to twelve months before the fateful decision gets made to cross over the line. In exceptional cases, this timeline can get compressed to weeks or even days.

STAGE THREE: THE CRISIS/CLIMAX/ RESOLUTION STAGE

When it gets to be just too much to bear, some people descend into meltdown mode, a mindset of panic, desperation, paralyzing anxiety, altered thinking, and impaired judgment. In a word, it's like drowning. To mentally cope and survive, these people will resort to various extreme defensive strategies. Many will enter into what I call a *Personal Bubble Psychology*, in which they will view the world in terms that are internally logical, coherent and consistent, but in terms of the real world, entirely very wrong. *Personal Bubble Psychology*, a private world unto itself, escapes the constraints of customary logic and judgment and is temporarily impenetrable to outside influence and reason. Within the bubble, everything makes perfect sense, is simple and compelling, and can reach the proportions of an epiphany. Common examples that are less pernicious include falling in love, or getting into a frenzy about buying a car or a house.

Insurmountable problems call for extreme survival measures, so the psychologically drowning person desperately searches for a miraculous solution. Within his *Personal Bubble Psychology*, new and dangerous ideas beckon, penetrating the mental storm and chaos with the alluring promise of fixing at one fell stroke everything that is wrong.

Alcoholism or even suicide may appear to be the perfect solutions for those who direct their energies in an inwardly dark direction. These choices may stir up trouble on the job (or even result in death), but do not necessarily create serious risk for espionage.

However, there are others who will choose to direct their energies outwardly and take action against others. Returning to the core psychology, *an intolerable sense of personal failure, as privately defined by that person*, they will need to deny their sense of inner failure and prefer to blame and project all their inner sense of badness outwardly onto others. In effect, they are saying, "It's not me that's the failure – it's them."

Context becomes important here. The prospective insider spy wants to project all his negative self-appraisal, self-disappointment and self-loathing onto local, handy targets. Perhaps he will abuse his wife or children. Or if he works for the proverbial Post Office, he could "go postal." Working within the intelligence community channels the rage and offers an obvious way to get back at the supposed oppressor that did him wrong: He can turn traitor. This usually comes to his mind as an epiphany. The angry prospective insider spy hopes to get back at

"them," eliminate his money worries, relieve pressures of all kinds, and solve everything in one brilliant plan.

And so the typical insider spy is not so much recruited by the skill of a hostile service intelligence officer but is rather self-recruited. Some insider spies have been known to energetically press for recruitment against the active resistance of the hostile intelligence service they chose to work for. Persevering in his efforts to overcome the skepticism of the hostile service – that fears getting suckered by a controlled dangle – he will make multiple contacts volunteering to spy, until he finally gets picked up.

STAGE FOUR: THE POST-RECRUITMENT STAGE

This is the honeymoon stage for the newly minted insider spy, and can last for one to several months. He feels relief, even euphoria. With his new plan underway, everything now is coming together and makes such good sense. Money worries are calmed. His new handler seems simpatico, respectful, and also shows the excellent judgment of genuinely appreciating his great worth. There are plenty of interesting activities to keep the novice insider spy quite busy, such as learning new tradecraft, and classified documents for him to steal and pass along to the other side. There is so much more to his life now than his boring old day job.

STAGE FIVE: THE REMORSE/ MORNING-AFTER STAGE

No crisis lasts forever, by definition. Any crisis and its associated reverberations will eventually settle down. The insider spy now has a chance to pause for reflection. His perspective will change as it becomes clearer what really happened to him during the course of his recent horrible crisis, and a kind of buyer's remorse can set in. His original decision to spy occurred under intense pressure cooker conditions, but his Remorse Stage can linger as a protracted, agonizing struggle. As the old saying goes: Act in haste, repent at leisure.

Personal Bubble Psychology abruptly terminates when rude reality punctures the bubble. The defining statement that retrospectively characterizes *Personal Bubble*

> "I am utterly amazed to find this [paper] that accurately describes the true experiences of the spy. Reading the stages actually made me tremble as I recalled my own entry into the world of espionage and the inevitable consequences." –Jens Karney (aka Jeffrey M. Carney) former US Air Force Intelligence Specialist and spy for the GDR's Ministry of State Security (MfS)

Psychology will now enter the mind of the insider spy: "What was I thinking?"

The insider spy can see that bad things did unfairly pile up on him back then — but now he wonders if he really did the right thing to turn traitor. Thus, his first doubts. Furthermore, now there is a dawning appreciation that he is stuck and trapped. With second thoughts about having crossed the line, fantasies crowd his mind about having a conversation with his handler to explain that it was all a terrible mistake. After further thought, he rules out that option. It would be like trying to get out of an arrangement with the Mafia. It would be very foolish, perhaps dangerous even to try.

What about doing the right thing and turning himself in? He could explain that he got overwhelmed and then did something very stupid, and could he please turn the clock back? On further thought, he realizes that option is impossible too. This situation is what I call Sharks in a Shark Tank. Sharks can swim nicely together, but if one of them gets nicked and starts to bleed, all the others will instantly turn to attack, predators going after prey. Given attitudes within the intelligence community, this course is also not a viable option, in fact, it's exceedingly dangerous: His career will be over for sure and jail time might be added too, constituting a total disaster not only for him but also for his innocent family. Bad as things are, better to leave things alone, keep spying, and hope for the best.

Now he is dealing with two failures. His first failure was being unable to manage his life during the time of crisis before he turned traitor. Now, being stuck and trapped, an existential black hole, what is he to make of being no longer in full charge of his own life? Is that not a second failure added to his first?

This appreciation of *stuckness* leads to the convergence of psychologies that unites most insider spies. While the individual psychologies of insider spies and the specifics of their unique life stories may have varied up to this point, these details no longer matter.

All insider spies now come to realize they are all in the same boat: stuck and trapped. Feeling stuck and trapped feels terrible, like being a bug pinned to a mat, robbing them of basic dignity and pride. They no longer are the captains of their own lives.

STAGE SIX: THE ACTIVE SPY CAREER STAGE

Resigned to trying to survive his messy existence, occasionally punctuated by moments of excitement,

challenge, and attempts at professionalism in the conduct of his "moonlighting job," the insider spy tries to just get on with it. Savoring to some degree his delicious secret life, at times feeling superior for it, he is mostly on the road to a life of dreary drudgery. Not only must he fulfill the requirements of his "day job," now he must also add on the rigors of his insider spy "moonlighting job."

And the insider spy must daily put up with the mental condition that all humans most dread: uncertainty. He never knows if and when he may be caught. He must always look over his shoulder and can never rest easy. He comes to realize that no matter how well he perfects his tradecraft, his ultimate survival depends more on luck than on skill. He cannot avoid thinking about how other insider spies were blown. Almost always it was because someone from "the other side," the side he secretly works for, decided to cross over to "our side" — with the damning information that disclosed the identities of the insider spies. He comes to understand that there is really no protection from this eventuality. It's like a time bomb forever ticking in his ears.

Thus, life becomes an endless nervous wait for the other shoe to drop. This grinding uncertainty is ceaseless and remorseless. Many a criminal subconsciously chooses to get caught, just to get it over with. So much for the glamour of the life of an insider spy.

STAGE SEVEN: THE DORMANCY STAGE(S)

From time to time, the insider spy just stops spying. He goes to ground, lies fallow, and quits producing. How perplexing for those who subscribe to the idea that insider spies are simply maliciously driven, robotically single-minded villains.

But how logical for Dormancy Stages to occur if the true psychology of the insider spy incorporates the conflicted dynamics described above. Life is nasty and brutish for the insider spy who has been at it for a few years. He feels burned out. The supposed solution to his original sense of failure and drowning years ago has transformed into a larger problem than ever before. Like the Sorcerer's Apprentice, his vaunted brilliant solution for his problems has mutated into a daily nightmare. Fantasies of escape from this daily dilemma abound. He thinks: "Maybe if I just dial down my productivity, perhaps they will forget about me? If I just keep quiet, I'll go off their radar screen — and then I'll resume my normal everyday life and pretend this never happened."

Then either his handler tugs on his leash or other stresses pile up again. Like an alcoholic, he goes back to the sauce. Many insider spies, such as Robert Hanssen and Earl Pitts, cycled through several Dormancy Stages.

STAGE EIGHT: THE PRE-ARREST STAGE

This is where unmistakable signs of surveillance get noticed by the insider spy. Finally the drama may be coming to its bad end. As mentioned, this development is almost always because of information carried over from "the other side." Later, counterintelligence officers will belittle the sloppy tradecraft exhibited by insider spies at this juncture. However, their observations are probably off the mark, for at this point, the insider spy is simply exhausted by the futility of the game. He has ceased to care about maintaining his tradecraft, and seeing his bad end clearly in sight, he just wants to get it over with. He will play out this drama to its bitter end. As unwelcome as getting caught will be, he will welcome relief from his grinding daily uncertainty.

STAGE NINE: THE ARREST AND POST-ARREST STAGE

Now the trap is sprung. The insider spy gets caught red-handed at the drop site. And out of his mouth come surly, arrogant remarks and teenager-like bravado and insolence. These are the comments and attitudes that commonly form the basis for making sense of insider spy motivation.

For example, immediately upon getting caught, Robert Hanssen said, "What took you so long?" These comments engender fury and outrage from within the intelligence and law enforcement communities, as well as from the general public. The insider spy's seeming lack of remorse and annoying nasty superiority actually covers up something entirely different.

The insider spy is now facing his third failure, added to his first two. He could not even succeed as a spy. He is now revealed to the entire world as a failure in this aspect of his life as well. It's like a flashback to his bad old days when he first felt like he was drowning. So he spits and fulminates like a teenage rebel without a cause, attempting to preserve his reputation, at least with himself, as a world-class desperado.

STAGE TEN: THE BROODING IN JAIL STAGE

Years go by, at least two or three. His fifteen minutes of notorious fame have long since passed. Incarcerated for all this time, the insider spy now broods, and forced by a lack of diversions, he must face himself for the first time. Gone are his insolence and his in-your-face comments, now replaced by more realistic, sadder but wiser self-observations about the way his life has gone wrong and the consequences of his poor choices. For example, interviews in print with Aldrich Ames conveyed such thoughts, and Robert Hanssen expressed similar thoughts of remorse and self-reproach directly to me.

> "There is nothing good that came as a result of my actions. I tried to serve two countries at the same time. That does not work."
> —Former Navy analyst and spy for Israel, Jonathan Pollard

Surprisingly, the insider spy is rarely truly dedicated to the subversion and destruction of his native land. His beef was always primarily with himself, and with the local people or institutions that were his nearby, handy targets. He may actually harbor attachment and true patriotic feelings towards his country, however paradoxical and unlikely it may seem. He now will offer gratuitous advice about how to protect the country from the likes of himself, and insightful ideas about the state of the world. Many of these ideas would be useful contributions – if only the jailed insider spy enjoyed the standing to be listened to and taken seriously.

This is the final stage, which provides the first real chance to get a balanced understanding of the perplexing life decision of someone who has decided to turn traitor.

THE EXISTENTIAL DILEMMAS OF THE INSIDER SPY

FAILURE UPON FAILURE

For a man, maintaining a stable sense of personal worth is key. However, the insider spy experiences three tremendous losses: He suffers two failures before getting caught: His first failure was his inability to successfully navigate his own life; his second failure was discovering that his best attempt to solve his worst life crisis turned out to be a pathetic delusion as he is now merely a puppet on the string of his handler. His third and very public failure is that he could not even succeed at being an insider spy.

STUCKNESS

This refers to the insider spy's condition of being in a state of paralysis, unable to steer the course of his own life. Caught between equally strong forces tugging in opposite directions, the net result is *stuckness*. This unhappy state of loss of control over his life undermines the insider spy's most fundamental bedrock of pride as a man.

CONVERGENCE OF PSYCHOLOGY

All insider spies wind up imprisoned by the same psychology: Fear of being caught; constant grinding uncertainty, waiting for the other shoe to drop; yearnings for deliverance and relief; despair and hopelessness about the ultimate direction their lives will take.

OTHER FACTORS

SOCIO-ECONOMIC PYRAMID

There are three layers within the pyramid of intelligence community personnel that provide guidance for understanding the nature of the life stresses that overwhelm prospective insider spies.

The base of the pyramid is the most densely populated layer, composed of enlisted military and blue-collar civilian employees in technical positions. Their troubling life issues are described well by country music lyrics: money woes, mean bosses, women who betray trust, and other basic life stresses. They are less well-screened when they enter on duty. While numerous, their access to classified materials is more limited, but collectively they can pass on to adversaries a voluminous amount of classified material, so insider spies from this layer can be very dangerous.

The middle layer, less numerous, is composed of scientific, technical, engineering, white-collar types from within the military branches as well as the civilian agencies. They enjoy greater accesses to classified materials. They are college graduates and their life problems tend to be the "mid-life crises" more typical of the middle class.

The topmost layer, smallest in number, is composed of the most highly screened professional intelligence officers. They enjoy the highest accesses and are privy to all-source intelligence. They represent the greatest threats if they decide to turn traitor, since they can disclose a great range of high-level strategic secrets. Their individual psychologies are more idiosyncratic and tend to be based on affronts to personal and professional pride.

GENDER DIFFERENCES

Insider spies are mostly males, but there are occasional women, too. The Core Psychology still applies but in a somewhat different way. Nearly all humans value two concerns at the top of the list of what everyone cares about: career success (including financial) and intimate relationships. On average, which of these two concerns holds the top position varies by gender. For men, career success tends to edge out intimate relationships. For women, the reverse tends to hold true.

Of course, this generalization is not etched in stone, and many exceptions do exist. This paper emphasizes male psychology simply because over 95% of insider spies are male. When women slip into becoming insider spies, it's often because of doubts about their worth as women and their attractiveness to the opposite sex. Hostile intelligence services have traditionally targeted women who seem vulnerable because of their loneliness. East German spy services used male "Ravens" to target female secretaries quite successfully.

CURRENT UNDERSTANDING AND PRACTICES

Conventional approaches to solving the problem of the insider spy have relied on careful screening at the time of first hire, follow-up background investigations, stringent security practices, and various high tech monitoring schemes.

Why don't these current practices work very well? Intelligence community personnel are sophisticated enough to realize that revealing details of serious life stresses, and the distress that results, is not a career-enhancing move. They will conceal as best they can any evidence of this. And they are good at it. Even so, distress can leak out, come to the attention of co-workers or management, and then action can be taken to refer them for appropriate help. These are not the cases of concern. The true cases of concern are those individuals who can preserve a calm outward demeanor while their private life descends into an awful pit. These types will never present themselves for help knowing all too well that

their careers would screech to a halt. Out of self-interest and having the talent for it, they are smart enough to dodge questioning that would reveal incriminating matters. Thus, the usual checks are not generally effective.

Attempts to study the problem have been frustrating. There is a dearth of formal official and academic studies of insider spy psychology partly because of the lack of easy access to the study material—the spies themselves. They are incarcerated and out of reach to researchers, except for those who work within the intelligence community or for those who work for private companies that have been cleared for such studies. The two main studies whose conclusions have been disseminated in a limited way (much of this work remains classified) are Project Slammer and the PERSEREC studies.

These studies have approached the problem by gathering voluminous demographic data, psychological testing, and interviews, to assemble a detailed accounting of the many disparate factors that seem to stand out as common factors. This has succeeded in painting an impressionistic picture of a group that numbers approximately 150 insider spies, constituting a very useful body of information. But these approaches also have methodological limitations since the formal instruments that were used can only go so far in digging beneath the surface of things to discern deeper psychological roots.

Also, the length of study of each subject seems to have been limited, which gets in the way of the chance to develop an in-depth personal relationship over an extended period of time. As a result, more subtle and deeper psychological dynamics do not surface and get examined. Furthermore, the information is somewhat undigested. There is little in the way of information that tracks the trajectory of the life of the insider spy from before the spying started until later.

These studies also lack a coherent overarching theory that could provide guidance for novel approaches to halt insider spying. Thus these studies, while correct, are also incomplete. They point to conclusions that may be overdrawn or disproportional in weight and importance.

For example, money is often emphasized as the chief motivating factor. I have shown that while money and greed may appear to be true motivations on the surface, deeper analysis points to more complex underlying dynamics. These studies can direct better profiling of those likely to commit espionage, or of those already

> The true cases of concern are those individuals who can preserve a calm outward demeanor while their private life descends into an awful pit.

engaged in it, but they primarily support the current exclusive emphasis on improving the detection strategies described above.

NEW DIRECTIONS PROPOSED

My work has suggested that further progress along the lines of better profiling and detection, while useful up to a point, faces limitations due to an iron law: the Law of Diminishing Returns. Each additional increment of effort costs more and more, with very little additional protection to show for it. Every news story detailing the capture of the latest insider spy seems to prove that human ingenuity can trump even the best efforts. Attempts to develop profiles that will predict who will become an insider spy have turned out to be blind alleys.

Because my work highlights the long-term dynamic evolution of the insider spy, it shifts emphasis away from pushing for intensified profiling and detection strategies. Instead, my work suggests strategies that favor new and different policies. These new policies would promote conditions that would make it less likely for someone to turn to spying in the first place, long before there's anything to detect. If already engaged in spying, new policies are suggested that make it more likely that insider spies would voluntarily turn themselves in.

A novel way to approach the problem of insider spying would be to build mechanisms that create safe exits for troubled insiders before they start to spy and safe exits for those already engaged in spying. While there would be difficult tradeoffs to calculate and manage, these novel approaches to fixing the problem of insider spies, while currently neglected in the United States, hold great promise for making our nation more secure.

Based upon the material presented here, I will be proposing a new proactive insider spy management paradigm called *NOIR*, which I believe will help diminish the dangerous threat of insider spying.

> "I regret the actions I took. They were wrong. They overshadowed anything good I've done in my life before and after. I'm glad it's over."
> —Former NSA employee and Russian spy David Boone

PART TWO
NOIR: PROPOSING A NEW POLICY FOR IMPROVING NATIONAL SECURITY BY FIXING THE PROBLEM OF INSIDER SPIES

A punch in the gut.

Intelligence professionals say this is what it felt like for them when they first heard that a fellow officer was all along an insider spy. They also felt stunned, infuriated, depressed, and of course, betrayed. Finally, they felt stupid for having missed it happening right under their noses, on their watch.

In the movie *Breach*, loosely based on the Robert Hanssen case, one FBI Special Agent assigned to counterintelligence bitterly stated that because of the losses due to Hanssen, as much as her career was devoted to strengthening national security, she "could have just stayed home."

Yet counterintelligence, the activity designed to thwart insider spying, has historically been the stepchild of the intelligence community. Positive intelligence, targeted at discovering our adversaries' secrets, has always been the intelligence community's fair-haired child, its most highly valued activity. Generally, that makes good sense.

Unfortunately, on too many occasions because of insider spying, advantages we were happy to gain as a result of our positive intelligence triumphs were annihilated. When a hostile intelligence service penetrates us, our adversary gets a low-cost "heads up" regarding not only our secrets, but also a great deal of what we know about their secrets. Goodbye, intelligence advantage. Worse, it gives them the opportunity to play us for fools. No wonder insider spying is a critical threat to our national security.

> Time and again, human ingenuity seems able to defeat the most stringent protection regimes.

Fixing the problem of insider spies has been frustrating. Conventional policies have proven less than satisfactory. There always seem to be more spies coming out of the woodwork. Efforts to improve matters have focused mainly on trying ever harder to develop profiles or other indicators for detecting potential or current insider spies, these days favoring high-technology methods.

While profiling has achieved its successes, the Law of Diminishing Returns enters the picture. Investing more and more into profiling and detection starts to approach limitations due to minimal added effectiveness, at the expense of rapidly escalating costs, which include negative impacts on workforce morale due to intrusiveness and false positives.

Time and again, human ingenuity seems able to defeat the most stringent protection regimes. For us to prevail over insider spying, we have room for improvement. There is room for something new.

If anything, recent events have increased the urgency. While the focus here will be on "classic" state-sponsored spying, the recent notorious "whistleblowers," Bradley Manning and Edward Snowden, have shown how easy it is to abscond with vast quantities of classified documents, given our reliance on electronic files. They went for one-time showy splurges of secrets, which is bad enough. Worse still are the usual practices of classic spies, who are still very busy out there.

Despite what intelligence professionals like to claim, they are not really in the business of stealing secrets.

KEY BENEFITS OF NOIR: TACTICAL AND STRATEGIC

THREE KEY TACTICAL BENEFITS:

1) CESSATION
Decisively stopping insider spying at much earlier stages.

2) MITIGATION
Getting more timely and thorough Damage Assessments, our greatest need from insider spies.

3) EXPLOITATION
Taking advantage of the cooperation of insider spies to work for us as doubled agents to feed disinformation, uncover other penetrations, etc.

THREE KEY STRATEGIC BENEFITS:

1) PREDOMINATION
Degrading spy-handler relationships of all adversary intelligence services, an advantage exclusive to our intelligence community, and our closest allies.

2) COORDINATION
Bridging stovepipes within the intelligence community by sharing a community-wide resource.

3) PREVENTION
Redefining the shared meaning of insider spying so no one will want to cross that line.

FIVE ANCILLARY BENEFITS OF *NOIR*

1) Partially Solving the Problem of the Non-Prosecutable Spy
2) Getting Traction with Ideological, Ethnic, Religious or Psychopathic Spies
3) Managing Difficult "Gray Zone" Personnel Problems
4) Creating an Employee Assistance Program (EAP) of Last Resort
5) Smoothing the Outplacement Process When All Else Fails

Stealing is actually grossly ineffective, since the victim knows what's been lost, and who likely stole it. True espionage is much more like embezzling. The victim doesn't know it's even happening, so it continues unabated. Reversing the notion of a "victimless crime," truly effective espionage produces a "crimeless victim."

This highlights the real challenge: how to protect our secrets when we don't know what secrets have been given away to our enemies by unidentified insider spies, working in the shadows for years on end with no outward drama.

Now, make room for something new.

The purpose of this paper will be to advance novel, probably controversial proposals for changing government policy to better manage the problem of insider spies. I consulted with and treated employees from all corners of the intelligence community for about twenty-five years, an immersion in the world of espionage. Along the way, I had the opportunity to be engaged as a consultant to the defense of three captured insider spies, including the notorious Robert Hanssen. Meeting in jail with all three, a couple of hours a week, each for a full year, afforded me the unique experience that opened windows into the minds of insider spies and contributed the basis for what follows.

This is Part Two of a two-part White Paper. Part One, entitled "True Psychology of the Insider Spy,"[1] provided the foundation for an enhanced understanding of the minds of insider spies. Ideally, it should be read first. Part One was published in the Fall 2010 issue of the AFIO's *Intelligencer* and is also posted on the Office of the National Counterintelligence Executive website (ncix.gov) and my website (NOIR4USA.org). The proposals advanced in this paper make use of the concepts put forward in Part One and flow logically from them.

NOIR'S MAIN AIMS: STOPPING SPYING. PREVENTING SPYING.

Taking guidance from the world of medicine, the concept of triage directs that attention be paid first to fixing immediately life-threatening conditions. Stopping insider spying, akin to stanching catastrophic but hidden hemorrhage, must be regarded as the most urgent concern, so this topic will be addressed in Section A.

Stopping insider spying must be rapidly followed by getting a thorough Damage Assessment. It cannot be overstated: a top quality Damage Assessment is absolutely crucial. Without it, how can the specific losses due to an insider spy's treachery be identified, much less mitigated?

Preventing insider spying, the second level of concern because it operates on a different time scale of urgency, will be addressed in Section B.

NOIR will stand as a quick reference term for all the

ideas and concepts presented in this paper. *NOIR* derives from the name of the proposed new government entity that would actually implement these ideas and concepts: the **National Office for Intelligence Reconciliation**. Details of *NOIR* will be addressed in Section C. (See the endnote for discussion of why the name, and its acronym *NOIR*, were chosen).[2]

SECTION A:
STOPPING SPYING

CONVERGENCE: CREATES THE OPPORTUNITY

Now for a surprise. It does not matter that much why spies originally decided to cross the line!

For stopping spying, for all of the findings described in Part One about the complex motivations of insider spies, ironically, it doesn't matter all that much. That's because crossing the line catapults all new spies into the same, shared position of feeling stuck, trapped, and terrified that at any time "the other shoe will drop." All insider spies come to understand that as soon as their identity gets leaked to us from within the foreign intelligence service they conspired to join – which can happen at any moment despite their best efforts at trade-craft – suddenly, their lives will turn to ruin. This forces all spies into a convergence of psychology. Even though there may be many psychological strands that lead to spying, inevitably they will get reduced to a single, shared psychology. Awareness of the phenomenon of convergence will make it easier to devise strategies and tactics to influence and persuade trapped spies to exit and come clean.

That said, the deeper understanding of what leads to the decision to cross the line, explored in Part One, is by no means useless knowledge. It will form the foundation for preventing spying, to be discussed later.

To help understand these dynamics, please examine the graphic on page 15 (reproduced from Part One), which delineates the Ten Life Stages of the Insider Spy. Note that the Ten Stages can vary as to how long each lasts, indicated by slanted hash marks. The bullets and asterisks will now begin to make sense. Stages that exhibit Convergence, starting with Stage 5, the Remorse Stage, are marked with asterisks. Convergence is what creates the opportunity for turning the tide of insider spying. The bullets will be discussed under Windows of Opportunity.

What if there were a way out?

RECONCILIATION: EXPLOITS THE OPPORTUNITY

When someone decides to step over the line to become an insider spy, as already noted, he now finds himself stuck and trapped. It dawns on him that he has no way out. He comes to realize it's unthinkable to beg to be released from his handler because too many bad things can happen. Think of the Mafia.

By the same token, to turn himself in to his home agency's security office offers no better prospects. Remember from Part One: Sharks in a Shark Tank.[3] The insider spy cannot expect to be welcomed back. More likely, he will face severe punishments leading to career termination and everyone in the intelligence community knows this.

Being stuck in this no-win situation causes the insider spy to resign himself to stay put, take his chances, and hope for the best. Lacking any viable alternatives, he is forced deeper into the arms of the hostile intelligence service that owns him. And the damages he inflicts on our national security accumulate year by year.

What if there were a way out? What if there were an alternative pathway so an insider spy could voluntarily turn himself in? What if there were a recognized, safe, government-sanctioned exit mechanism?

Imagine such a thing.

Currently, there is no word for an insider spy voluntarily turning himself in. There never has been a need for such a word because, as explained, it virtually never happens. For this nearly unknown event, we will adopt an existing word, *reconciliation*, and give it this new meaning. (See the endnote discussion as to why this particular word was chosen).[4]

If *reconciliation* were made available, what could possibly motivate an insider spy to consider it? The single most important motivator would be that he will not be sentenced to prison. From the perspective of an insider spy, prison would be a deal-breaker.

Before the reader collapses from cardiac arrest, please understand that *reconciliation* stipulates that all other punishments be left on the table. *Reconciliation* would have to be a highly conditional way out.

For example, the *reconciled* insider spy would, of course, have to lose his job within the intelligence community. He would have to promptly submit to an extremely thorough Damage Assessment. He would have to permanently lose his security clearance. He would have to fully pay back all funds illegally gained.

He would have to accept lifetime financial scrutiny. He would perhaps have to pay fines. He would perhaps have to adopt another identity. He would perhaps have to relocate and be cut off from family and friends (similar to the Witness Protection Program—WITSEC). He would perhaps have to suffer other punishments.

Furthermore, the *reconciliation* option would not be on offer to all spies. Certainly not to ones caught the conventional way. *Reconciliation* would only add an alternative, parallel pathway that would supplement, definitely not replace, current practices that include detection, surveillance, arrest, trial and long prison sentences. *Reconciliation* would be reserved only for insider spies not yet identified, who decide to voluntarily turn themselves in.

Reconciliation would be adding another tool to the arsenal.

Implementation of the *reconciliation* process would be conducted by a new, small, independent intelligence entity whose name has already been mentioned: the National Office for Intelligence Reconciliation. *NOIR* would be meant to serve the entire intelligence community, so perhaps it would make sense to come under the Office of the Director of National Intelligence (the ODNI), or the Office of the National Counterintelligence Executive (the ONCIX).

Aside from *reconciliation*, other *NOIR* functionalities, to be discussed, could spring from making available this new, shared community resource.

Why would an insider spy accept the litany of punishments listed above – except for prison – and still seriously consider *reconciliation*?

SEVEN FACTORS DRIVING FOR RECONCILIATION

1: UNCERTAINTY—PERPETUAL TORMENT FOR INSIDER SPIES

The very worst mental state is uncertainty. Bad news is never welcome. However, after the initial shock, we can eventually accept even very bad news. We can begin to conceive of plans to deal with our new, difficult circumstances. By contrast, uncertainty leaves us twisting slowly in the wind, with no clear direction. We can't plan.

Anxiety, tension, and dread grow in our imaginations, and our energy drains away.

The agonies of uncertainty are the daily fare for any insider spy. Even if he considers his tradecraft to be brilliant, the insider spy comes to realize that his fate actually depends not so much on his tradecraft prowess, but rather more so on sheer luck. That's because virtually all insider spies get disclosed when someone from the other side decides whether and when to cross over to our side. This new arrival, having to prove his *bona fides*, will reveal the identities of his intelligence service's recruited agents-in-place, the ones we consider the traitors in our midst.

Since the timing of this is never predictable, the insider spy lives in a constant state of uncertainty, paranoia and anxiety that when he least expects it, he will hear the proverbial "knock on the door."

To get a sense of this, imagine what it's like for any of us having to wait only a few short days for test results telling us whether we must face the diagnosis of cancer. Now, multiply that uncertainty and dread by hundreds of times, spread over the course of years. That's the truth of what's constantly in the mind of an insider spy.

> "When I first got into it, I didn't realize what it all meant. As I was doing it, I did come to realize and I did try to withdraw numerous times. I've lived a life of terror for 30 years that this whole thing would get found out."
> —Former NSA employee Robert Lipka, who spied for the KGB in the 1960s but was only caught in the 1990s.

Actually, this is not news to our offensive team in the field, our clandestine case officer cadre. One of the most important jobs for any case officer handling agents that we have recruited is to constantly reassure them that every measure is being taken to protect their safety. Our agent can get spooked at any time because of his nagging fears and doubts – and there goes our valuable asset. So we already know from this alternative perspective how much worry about disclosure eats away at the minds of recruited agents.

2: STUCKNESS

Feeling profoundly stuck, trapped and helpless is an ego destroyer for the insider spy. History shows that the vast majority of insider spies are men. *Stuckness* goes right against male pride and dignity. The insider spy no longer feels in charge of his life, no longer the captain of his destiny. He would do nearly anything to get unstuck – if it were safe to do so. Sun Tzu said: Always leave your enemy an exit.

3: BURNOUT AND EXHAUSTION

The stress and strain of leading a double life requires a level of energy that wanes with age. During Stage 4, the Post-Recruitment Stage, it may seem fun, exhilarating, filled with a secret sense of superiority. ("I-know-some-thing-you-don't-know.") However, over time, the risk factors associated with spying begin to nag at the mind. If the operation were to go sour, the only one truly at-risk is the insider spy. Not his handler, who typically enjoys diplomatic immunity.

The recruited agent gets exhausted. He's got his day job to do, plus the time demands of his secret calling. Tradecraft, rather than an exciting, fun proposition, becomes an unpleasant reminder of the fix he's in. Eventually, he starts to make excuses to avoid it, he procrastinates, until his handler yanks his chain and reluctantly, he has to go back at it – which explains Stage 7, the Dormancy Stage(s). Spying began as a survival strategy, a seemingly perfect solution for his out-of-control inner life crisis. Now, the solution has mutated into an even bigger problem. Scary, and also, sheer drudgery.

4: LONELINESS

A spy is the loneliest person in the world. There is no one who fully knows what's on his plate. He dares not reveal the secret compartments of his life to anybody, even (especially?) his wife. That's why a spy's handler has such a hold. The handler seems to be such a sympathetic listener. He is the only one who knows about the spying. He showers praise on the insider spy for his productivity. However, that begins to wear thin as the insider spy senses that his handler's high regard is not authentic. He comes to believe that mostly he's being used and played. So it's back to loneliness.

5: SHIFT OF VALUES

Spying is a young man's game. Past forty, the world begins to look different. What the insider spy once considered acceptable risk he now sees as reckless. Relationships with his spouse and children, once relegated behind career excitements on his hierarchy of valued things now become more important. The truth begins to sink in that he is not invulnerable. If he got caught, he would risk losing daily contact with his loved ones. Now and then, he's bound to come across news stories about other spies who did get caught – putting the lie to reassurances from his handler that he is absolutely safe. He really could get blown. Then what?

And all this to what purpose? His original reasons for turning to spying no longer seem so convincing. Even ideological beliefs that in his youth seemed so transcendent now seem ridiculous. Countries other than his own that he once viewed as morally superior begin to look less admirable. He begins to feel like a fool. And a tool. Imagine having to explain to his grown children the convoluted, antiquated motives of his youth – after he's caught.

6: HONOR AND PATRIOTISM (!)

Another surprise. The insider spy seriously considers himself to be a patriotic American. Old-fashioned traditional values that were imbued in him in grade school stay alive within his heart. The insider spy's beef was usually never with our country. His beef was really with himself. At his weakest moment, his way of handling overwhelming stress was to project his self-disappointment and anger onto the nearest handy target, typically his home agency. As Tip O'Neill famously said: "All politics is local."

Years later in jail, the insider spy will spontaneously give voice to his residual patriotism. He will be full of advice about how to improve things in our country, including how to protect our nation from the likes of himself. His gratuitous advice is hard to take seriously, so it's easy to dismiss this patriotic impulse as merely an artifact of capture. It shouldn't be dismissed.

> "I regret very much the betrayal of the trust they put in me, and of the oaths that I swore, and that I did it for my own gain and then my own arrogance."
> —Former CIA officer and Russian spy Rick Ames

The theme of an American who temporarily gets overtaken by a spasm of disloyalty, which is then followed by a rueful return to his senses, is not new. It has been addressed in a number of works of literature, such as *The Man Without A Country* and *The Devil and Daniel Webster*.[5]

7: HOPE

Hope does spring eternal. The insider spy cannot abandon the dream of starting over and getting to make different choices. He can't help wondering: "Will it ever be possible for me to live a normal life again?"

Ten Life Stages of the Insider Spy

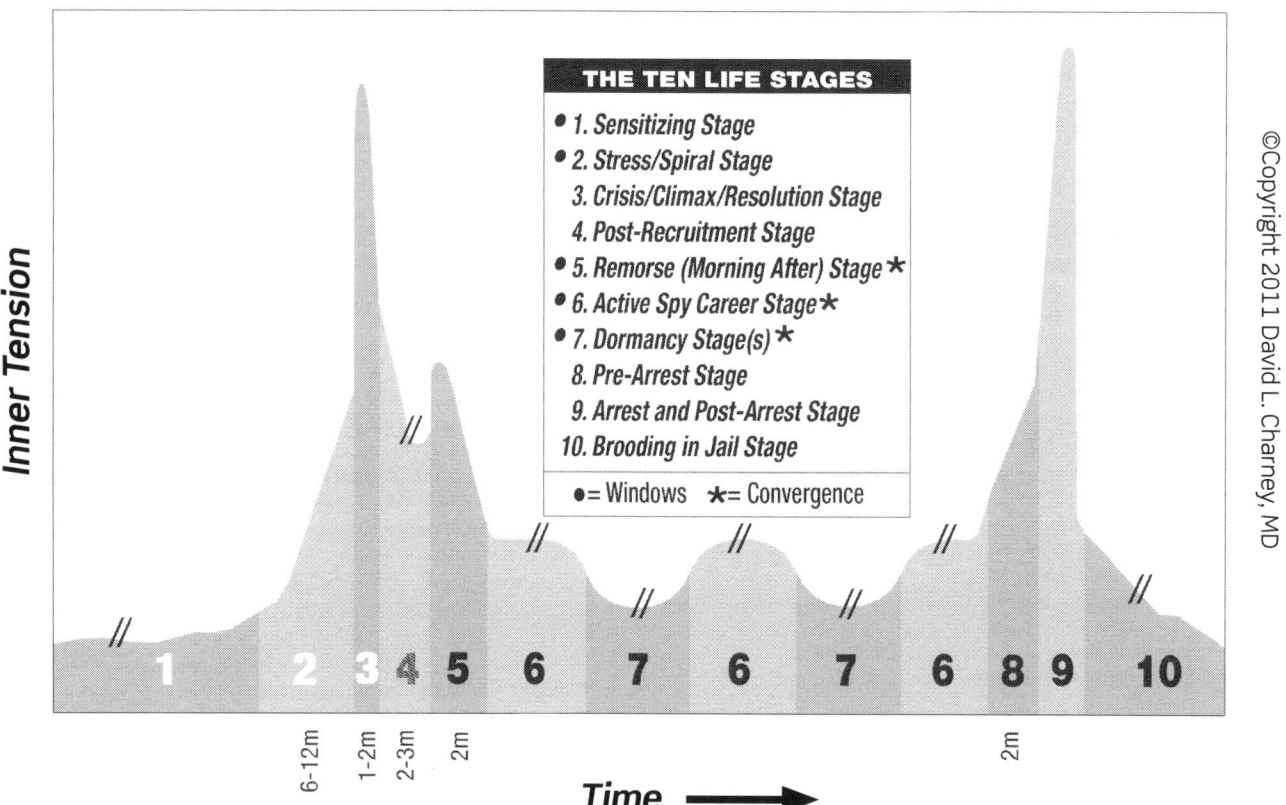

Inner Tension

THE TEN LIFE STAGES

- 1. *Sensitizing Stage*
- 2. *Stress/Spiral Stage*
- 3. *Crisis/Climax/Resolution Stage*
- 4. *Post-Recruitment Stage*
- 5. *Remorse (Morning After) Stage* ★
- 6. *Active Spy Career Stage* ★
- 7. *Dormancy Stage(s)* ★
- 8. *Pre-Arrest Stage*
- 9. *Arrest and Post-Arrest Stage*
- 10. *Brooding in Jail Stage*

● = Windows ★ = Convergence

1 2 3 4 5 6 7 6 7 6 8 9 10

6-12m 1-2m 2-3m 2m 2m

Time ⟶

WINDOWS OF OPPORTUNITY

Inspecting the graphic of the Ten Life Stages of the Insider Spy once again, some Stages are opportune for *reconciliation* and some are blackout periods. The windows are either Open (bulleted in the graphic), or Closed.

Stage 1 is so long ago, that for our purposes, it's water under the bridge.

Stage 2 is the best time for prevention strategies.

Stages 3 and 4 are too feverish and chaotic for prevention or *reconciliation*.

Stage 5 is the first Stage when convergence comes into play, and is the first open window for *reconciliation*.

Stages 5, 6 and 7 are the ideal target Stages for *reconciliation* operations, especially during the handoff of the insider spy to a new handler.

Stages 8, 9 and 10 are too late for *reconciliation*.

NOIR PACKAGE OF CALIBRATED PUNISHMENTS AND CONDITIONAL PROTECTIONS WITH KICK-OUT PROVISIONS

NOIR recognizes that the risks of insider spying are the costs of doing business in the world of intelligence — then moves on to the next logical question: "Now what?"

With *reconciliation*, the insider spy turns himself in and must cooperate in delivering a full, complete, and truthful Damage Assessment — but he does not go to prison. This deal is an inducement for the spy to voluntarily turn himself in. Otherwise, it is safer for him to stay put. He will be spared the worst punishment — prison. He will spare his family (and his home agency!) shame and humiliation because there will be no public disclosure.

However, it will not be cost-free to him. *NOIR* cannot be a "Get Out of Jail Free Card." He will have to endure many of the punishments that were listed above. Every punishment should be on the table — short of prison.

The punishments would have to be calibrated, in the sense that they must be noxious enough to satisfy interested government parties, and the general public, that the deal is not too lenient; but the punishments must not be overly harsh either. They must be acceptable enough to the insider spy so that he can view them as a reasonable payback to society, offering him the way out he so desperately desires – for all seven of the important reasons mentioned above.

The punishments must also be designed so that they can stay hidden; otherwise, certain advantages that benefit the United States would get compromised. For example, the chance to orchestrate double agent operations.

Initiating the *reconciliation* process will be a delicate matter, such as establishing first contact with *NOIR* that is safe and secure, followed by a negotiation of surrender terms. Some flexibility regarding the terms of the package will have to be factored in, which will call for exercising judgment.

A major government benefit will be the getting of a timely, rapid and thorough Damage Assessment. This is where *NOIR* can shine. In conventional scenarios, there is a Kabuki dance of negotiation between government prosecutors and defense attorneys. The government threatens capital punishment for the spy, and severe punishment for the spouse as a knowing accomplice, but everyone knows how this plays out. Ever since the case of the Rosenbergs sixty years ago, we have not resorted to capital punishment. It usually ends up that the spouse gets off relatively lightly, and the captured spy agrees to accept a long prison sentence and to fully cooperate with the Damage Assessment.

With this playbook, realistically, there's a problem with the Damage Assessment. Once the usual deal is done, the insider spy has nothing much more to lose, so he just grudgingly goes through the motions. Truly full, reliable cooperation is questionable. This dynamic will improve appreciably given *NOIR* kick-out provisions.

If at any time it's discovered that the *reconciled* insider spy lied, withheld important information, or otherwise did not fully conform to his *reconciliation* agreement, then his protection from imprisonment can be withdrawn, and he will face public disclosure. Now the spy really has

NOIR

NATIONAL OFFICE FOR INTELLIGENCE RECONCILIATION

something to lose – a much more powerful incentive for true cooperation.

NOIR: IMPLEMENTS THE OPPORTUNITY

Why a New, Independent Entity Is Needed

Reconciliation must take into account the psychological realities of the target population. For the core function of *reconciliation*, the targets are resentful, disaffected, disgruntled intelligence community employees who are angry with and distrustful of their home agencies. Their original need was to project outwardly their intolerable sense of personal failure, and it was convenient for them to zero in on their home agency as the nearest, handiest scapegoat ("All politics is local"). They had no problem collecting plenty of grievances to justify their revenge since innumerable instances of mistreatments routinely occur in any bureaucracy.

Insider spies have nursed negative attitudes towards their home agencies. It's a non-starter for them to seek sanctuary from a representative of their despised agencies.

Thus, for *reconciliation* to start on a solid footing requires an off-premises neutral entity to sidetrack these raw emotions. Using the separation and distance provided by a supportive, neutral third party to smooth the exit of difficult employees is a concept well understood in the world of private industry.

Insider spies from within any of the existing sixteen intelligence community agencies will find it preferable to voluntarily turn themselves in to this new, specialized office precisely because it is not their home agency. *NOIR* can serve this purpose for all of the intelligence community agencies, cutting across stovepipes, and fulfilling one of the three strategic benefits claimed for *NOIR* at the beginning of this paper: Coordination.

It might be assumed that the FBI would be the natural place to house *NOIR* functions, but that's not so. Two of the three insider spies interviewed by me, both Special Agents of the FBI, said that if it had been available, they would have considered *reconciliation*. However, for the reasons listed above, they also made it clear there was no chance they would have dared to *reconcile* with a component of their home agency, the FBI.

We can surmise that if there were more insider spies from within the FBI interested in *reconciliation*, they would only consider doing it through an office outside the FBI.

It probably would not be practical for the FBI to serve the *NOIR* function for all the other agencies except for itself. Thus, *NOIR* should be separate from the FBI, and it should serve all the other intelligence agencies, including the FBI.

Also, by history and culture, the FBI has been and must continue to be the fearsome hunter and prosecutor of spies, not the welcoming refuge for spies who want to voluntarily call it quits. Let the fierce FBI team stay in character. To be both "Good Cop" and "Bad Cop" would be to weaken its strengths of purity of focus and concentration, and be confusing to all.

As a useful appliance within the intelligence community, let *NOIR* act as another feeder mechanism into the FBI. Let *NOIR*, using its novel and different methodology, reel insider spies into the FBI, which can then play to its strengths. The FBI is brilliant at thoroughly following up with cases, rolling up spy networks, solving linked cases, running double agent operations, etc. With an independent *NOIR* taking the lead for *reconciliation* operations, the FBI loses nothing; it comes out ahead by getting to do even more of its proper work.

Once the proposed new entity, *NOIR*, the National Office for Intelligence Reconciliation is stood up, it can also take on other, linked functions that further its two prime missions: stopping and preventing insider spying. *NOIR* would serve the entire intelligence community in those two roles and not have any other intelligence missions. It would be another tool in the toolbox. Even in name, *NOIR* would not presume to be a Three Letter Agency.

NOIR would not replace counterintelligence activities within any other agency. Those security components understand best their own agency's culture and must continue to energetically pursue their usual internal detection efforts. *NOIR* would have no direct role in positive intelligence activities.

NOIR would specialize in offering insider spies its parallel, alternative safe exit pathway only for those prepared to embark upon the *reconciliation* track, and accepting its demanding conditional provisions.

TEN RATIONALES FOR NOIR

1: GETTING REAL ABOUT HOW INSIDER SPIES ARE CAUGHT

Historically, spy-hunters in counterintelligence components are not all that successful at detecting spies on their own in a timely manner. In almost all cases, spies are revealed because of defections from the other side. Where spy-hunters do shine is after spies get caught, by executing thorough Damage Assessments and by ferreting out links to other spies or spy networks. Because of this, spy-hunters are often frustrated, reduced to waiting and hoping for the next break in a case. But as they say, "Hope is not a strategy."

From a strategic perspective, the exertions of spy-hunters amount to a passive mode of operating. It can take years before a lucky defection breaks a case. Meanwhile, the losses remain invisible, with only faint whiffs indicating something's amiss; as mentioned, effective espionage is more like embezzling than stealing.

By contrast, *NOIR* would be proactive in that it changes the rules of the spy game in favor of the United States. *NOIR* resets the internal calculations of the insider spy, and forces him to reconsider his ill-advised decision. In effect, *NOIR* lowers barriers to exit by freeing up the stuck condition of the insider spy, driving him to take action to bail out of his nerve-wracking spy life.

2: BROADENING EMPHASIS FROM DETECTION TECHNOLOGY TO HUMAN PSYCHOLOGY

NOIR emphasizes the individual psychology of the insider spy, his internal world, how he sees things. This contrasts with current practice with its greater emphasis on external perspectives that spring out of the Law Enforcement Mindset, including policing, detection methods based on high technology, polygraphing, stern threatening messages, controls and punishments.

This external perspective is time-honored, proven and effective – but only up to a point. If used as the only approach, it leaves cards on the table that could be played more effectively. Instead of relying exclusively on external pressure tactics, we can add the additional *NOIR* mechanism that works mainly on the internal track, the mind of the spy. We can readjust the thinking of the insider spy to want to come back to us, of his own accord, and with less effort and expense.

Current policies are necessary but not sufficient. Law enforcement professionals may conclude that this line of argumentation disparages tough stances towards managing the problem of insider spies, or proposes weakening such policies. This could not be further from the truth. If anything, *NOIR* prefers even harsher measures – for insider spies caught the conventional way.

Consider shepherding dogs that drive sheep into the pen. They harass the sheep with frightening charges and vicious barking from all directions – except where the pen is located – so there's no place else to go that's safe. Similarly, *NOIR* fully favors retaining today's stringent policies because they exert herding pressure on insider spies that will make *reconciliation* through *NOIR* all the more attractive.

3: SHIFTING THE PARADIGM TO A HIGHER NATIONAL SECURITY MINDSET

With a National Security Mindset the highest priority is to neutralize existential threats that genuinely endanger national survival. A competing mindset is the Law Enforcement Mindset, employing classic detection to expose insider spies, no matter how long it may take, with the end result of maximum punishment. This competition of values is vexing since both mindsets have their merits, though they aren't mutually contradictory. Still, a clear-eyed choice must be made. *NOIR* takes the position that the National Security Mindset must prevail. With this priority kept firmly in mind, shutting down insider spying, getting the critical Damage Assessment, and attaining both goals sooner rather than later, are seen as more important than preserving traditional approaches.

Compare the situation to a hostage-taking scenario. A trained negotiation team will rush to the scene, knowing that at the end of the day, their number one goal must be that the hostage comes out alive. They would be professionally pleased if the hostage-taker gets captured or killed. However, if the hostage-taker somehow gets away – but the hostage ends up alive and well – that's still a good day. Insider spies are like hostage-takers. They hold our national security hostage. If we can neutralize them, even at the cost of less than maximum but still significant and appropriate punishment, that's still a good day.

4: GAME THEORY IDEAS

In Game Theory, conflicted situations are studied. Maximizing outcomes for the players is the goal. Studies show that players come out ahead when they give up complete triumph over their adversaries in favor of somewhat more balanced outcomes. While not optimal for any player, over many iterations of a game, players do come out best when they forego big wins and settle for lesser ones. There are many practical applications of this thinking, including the situation of insider spies.

5: IDEAS FROM ECONOMICS; THE COSTS OF SPYING

There are costs to everything, a cardinal principle of economics. There is no such thing as a free lunch. Costs may be hidden, but they are always there. When comparing policies, it's important to identify all the costs so that decision makers are fully informed. With current insider spy policy it's taken for granted that only detection and severe punishments have any place.

There are costs to this position. For starters, detection is generally unsuccessful in uncovering spies. Success in ferreting out spies usually boils down to waiting and to luck. Usually, insider spies get disclosed by someone from the controlling intelligence service who decides to come over to our side. Every spy who is not caught and who enjoys a long tenure risks damaging us on the scale of a Rick Ames, or of a Robert Hanssen, or of the Walker family gang, costing US taxpayers billions of dollars and lives lost.

Worse, in wartime, secrets disclosed to our adversaries may result in losses of thousands of military personnel and billions of dollars worth of hardware assets. If only one spy of the scale mentioned above were stopped, that would spare us immense damage. To exaggerate, current policy says: "It's OK for us to lose $100 billion, and thousands of lives, so long as if we ever catch that traitor-bastard spy – we put him behind bars for life!"

Obviously, the longer a spy's tenure, the worse the losses suffered. With *reconciliation*, the insider spy exits much earlier from his treasonous career with fewer valuable intelligence losses. From an economic cost/benefit perspective, we must account for all the losses due to spying, a mix of hard costs with dollar signs attached, and soft costs that are expensive, but lack easily attached dollar signs.

The costs:

- Loss of sources and methods
- Loss of compromised CIA case officers – their careers are blown
- Loss of timely options to mitigate problems due

to delayed Damage Assessments

- Loss of good reputation for recruiting new agents, given perceived loss of safety

- Rebuilding betrayed networks, both human and technical

- Options for double agent and disinformation operations

- Foreign recruited agents who are jailed or killed

- Detecting, investigating, arresting, and prosecuting at trial

- Incarceration for many years

- Loss of Agency morale and reputation when the story gets out. In the aftermath of the revelation of an insider spy, there's long-term agency turmoil, with loss of cohesion and focus. Energy gets wasted on recriminations; focus gets inwardly directed vs. mission-oriented.

- Loss of general public's confidence in the competence of the affected agency

Many, though not all of these costs would be reduced or disappear with *reconciliation*. To be fair, new costs would be added, such as the costs of standing up *NOIR* to implement *reconciliation*. *NOIR*'s costs will be comparatively cheap.

6: IDEAS FROM INSURANCE

Protecting valuable assets by purchasing insurance coverage is well understood and routine. Annual premiums are usually a very small percentage of the full value of the covered asset. Is the cost of "laying off risk," as they say in the insurance industry, a good tradeoff to make? You can "go bare," but don't cry if the worst happens. Often, it's not a matter of choice. Try to obtain a mortgage on your house without complying with your lender's demand for an acceptable level of insurance.

Setting up the proposed *NOIR* mechanism will be hard and also costly (but there are ways to limit costs, described later). Costs to fund *NOIR* should be viewed as an insurance premium that offsets the risk of paying for the immense costs of rebuilding potentially scores

"It's OK for us to lose $100 billion, and thousands of lives, so long as if we catch that traitor-bastard spy—we put him behind bars for life!"

of billions of dollars of lost intelligence assets.

To sharpen the point about the issue of trading off insurance costs (*NOIR*), against the catastrophic costs of espionage, imagine a genie appears with this offer: "I'm willing to turn the clock back to just before Snowden (or Walker, Pelton, Ames or Hanssen), gave away all your precious secrets. You won't have lost any of them! How much would you be willing to pay?"

7: ISSUES OF SCALE: WHY SIZE MATTERS

Taking into account the scale of things, in some matters, scaling up the size of things changes how we think about them. It becomes not just a difference in degree; it becomes a difference in kind. Remember the Banker's Story: If you owe the bank $50,000, you can't sleep at night. If you owe the bank $5,000,000, the banker can't sleep at night.

Consider reprehensible crimes, such as murder, rape, etc. Though terrible, even when they scale up to numerous victims, such as with serial murderers, to be cold-blooded about it, they can be thought of as "retail" crimes. The scale of these crimes falls short of crimes that reach "wholesale" proportions, such as with a 9/11 event. When hundreds or thousands of lives are lost, it becomes a difference in kind. We are forced to rethink things when the scale of a problem ramps up exponentially. With espionage, the potential for harm to the entire nation is so great, such as mass loss of life and treasure, as with a 9/11 catastrophe or with a war situation, that taking new, otherwise unthinkable measures can gain credence.

Insider spying, which potentially exposes our nation to scaled-up existential risk, requires us to consider remedies that may be a stretch. To waive prison as a punishment for insider spying, as proposed by *NOIR's reconciliation*, may be objectionable. If as a result we're spared horrific national scale consequences, it's a remedy that can be justified.

8: GOOD COP/BAD COP, CARROTS AND STICKS

Good Cop/Bad Cop is age-old practical wisdom, used because it works. By contrast, with insider spies today, there's only the Bad Cop. We also need the Good Cop component. *NOIR* provides the missing Good Cop.

This concept is not new and we're using it now. It's how we destroyed the Mafia. We used WITSEC the same way: making it safe for mobsters to bail out so we could get what we wanted more: taking down the mob. In its day, WITSEC faced a difficult uphill battle before getting stood up. To achieve our desired larger goal, it finally made sense to make the tradeoff. Espionage ranks worse than the Mafia as a threat to the safety of our nation. While we strongly value bringing criminals to justice, our collective national security is too important for us to limit options. We need to do what will work.

It's the same as using both the carrot and the stick. Right now, with insider spies, it's all stick but no carrot. *NOIR* supplies the missing carrot.

9: TRADEOFFS: THE BUSINESSMAN'S CHOICE

In any buying decision, a businessman gets to pick only two of the following three key factors: Quality, Speed and Price. For example, buying a new car with exactly the options we want. The dealer says: "We can get the car you want (Quality) at a good low Price, but you'll have to wait two months for the factory to build it." We give up Speed in favor of Quality and Price. The dealer continues: "But we have a car on our lot with nearly all the options you want. We'll give you a great low price and you can drive it off the lot right now – so long as you're OK with cloth upholstery instead of the premium leather." Now, we're giving up Quality in favor of Speed and better Price.

Translating this in terms of factors relevant to insider spies: Quality means a full, rapid and complete Damage Assessment; Speed means how quickly the insider spy quits; Price means the spy's punishment, the harsher the better (in this case we seek the highest rather than the lowest price). According to the Businessman's Choice, we get to pick only two of these three key factors.

Current policy selects for Price (we go for the harshest sentence), gives up on Speed (it could take decades before the insider spy gets identified), and Quality (of the Damage Assessment, which can vary, depending on true cooperation. Once a life sentence is imposed on the insider spy, what more can the government use as

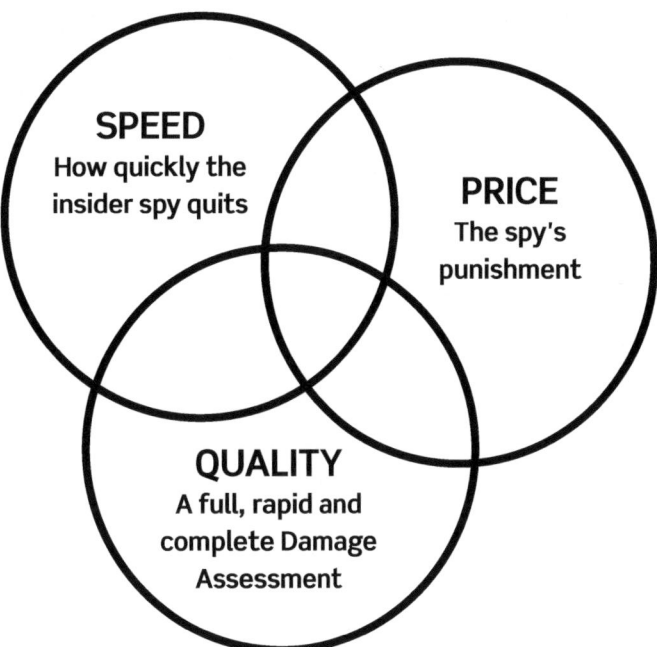

According to the Businessman's Choice, we get to pick only two of these three key factors.

leverage to force truly full cooperation?)

Is this tradeoff really in the national security interest? Are we really satisfied that adding 10 or 20 years to a spy's sentence is worth all the losses that the country might suffer, strategic and perhaps even existential, if spying continues unimpeded for a couple of decades or more? With several infamous insider spies, the financial losses alone amounted to tens of billions of dollars when all the costs of undoing the damages and rebuilding replacement intelligence systems got added up. Also, there were the incalculable costs of agents' lives lost, as well as the degradation of the intelligence community's morale, reputation and ability to function effectively.

Applying the Businessman's Choice concept to insider spying, there's a clear advantage when Speed (getting the insider spy out of the game more quickly), gets ranked over Price (harshest prison sentence). With *reconciliation*, Quality (of the Damage assessment) improves too.

10: SPIRIT, MORALITY AND VALUES

■ *SPIRIT OF NOIR*

NOIR doesn't offer the option of *reconciliation* in the spirit of forgiveness. Nor out of compassion, sympathy, empathy, or other sweet sentiments. *Reconciliation* comes out of a deeper understanding of the mind of the insider spy. However, *NOIR* also appreciates: To understand is not to condone.

Reconciliation is put forward purely out of national self-interest: to limit and mitigate the unacceptable costs of prolonged insider spying. A tradeoff is accepted. The moral satisfaction of maximally punishing treasonous spies is exchanged for an invaluable Good: the overall improved strategic security of the entire nation.

NOIR represents a real shift in the paradigm. *NOIR's* policies run counter to the wish to satisfy citizens' moral outrage directed against spies by seeking the most severe punishments. Remember that *NOIR's* treatment of spies is strictly limited to those who voluntarily turn themselves in. The paradigm shift in this case is extremely conditional.

■ MORAL VS. MORALISTIC VIEWS

Moral views look to achieving good ends from the perspective of the big picture and the long view. Moralistic views generally seem to take a short-term view, never mind the bigger picture. *NOIR* claims a basis in the moral as opposed to the moralistic view.

Military field commanders in wartime must face similar moral calculations. They must send soldiers into battle, in some instances knowing full well that they will be sacrificing the few to achieve larger goals that will save the many. *NOIR* looks to preserving long-term national security as being more important than exacting the most severe punishments for spies – but only if they voluntarily turn themselves in.

■ LENIENCY

To suppose that *NOIR* advocates a kinder, gentler attitude towards the treatment of spies in general would be a serious misreading of its thrust. In fact, *NOIR* advocates no such thing for caught spies. Maintaining the status quo of severe punishments for spies caught the conventional way is actually a critical element of *NOIR*. *NOIR* needs the current stringent policies to remain in place for it to work at all. *NOIR* effectiveness relies on the proven twin pillars of The Good Cop and The Bad Cop, or The Carrot and The Stick.

Current doctrine and practice, reliance on only one pillar, is criticized by *NOIR* as the key shortcoming – because it doesn't work very well. *Reconciled* spies are the only class of spies that *NOIR* is prepared to safeguard with its protections. *NOIR* protections are not intended to be nice. The relatively less punitive treatment to be offered exclusively to *reconciled* spies is the small price

that the nation will pay for the advantages gained in national security.

■ DETERRENCE

If current policies were working so well, how come there never seems to be a shortage of new spies? Perhaps some spies do get deterred, but at what cost? Granting that *NOIR* may reduce deterrence to some degree, it would be counterbalanced by the benefits that *NOIR* would confer.

NOIR is not a "Get Out of Jail Free Card." While jail gets relinquished as a punishment for *reconciling* spies, a variety of other serious punishments must be a part of the package that a spy must accept. *NOIR* does preserve deterrence because any spy caught conventionally is still subject to severe punishments. *NOIR* is by no means pushing for leniency for all spies. In fact, *NOIR* advocates unequivocally that severe punishments for caught spies must be preserved for *NOIR* to work.

■ APPEALS TO AN INSIDER SPY'S RESIDUAL VALUES

Surprisingly, many spies harbor an abiding love of country, still viewing themselves as patriotic Americans. Therefore, consider this motto for *NOIR*:

Come back. Your country still needs you.

■ A PROVOCATIVE QUESTION FOR COUNTERINTELLIGENCE PROFESSIONALS:

Do you love your country more than you hate these spies?

BENEFITS OF NOIR

The benefits of *NOIR* can be divided into two categories: Tactical and Strategic. Tactical refers to benefits that derive from improvements in the management of individual insider spy cases. Strategic refers to improvements in the world of espionage writ large.

TACTICAL BENEFITS OF *NOIR*

CESSATION

Cessation means getting insider spies to cease their spying, sooner rather than later. The special contribution of *reconciliation*: creation of a mechanism, for the first time, that provides a credible, safe way out for stuck insider spies.

MITIGATION

Owing to the *reconciliation* agreement, we get a more rapid and complete Damage Assessment, with teeth ensuring real cooperation.

EXPLOITATION

The *reconciled* insider spy can participate in double agent operations, can feed disinformation, and otherwise manipulate hostile services.

STRATEGIC BENEFITS OF *NOIR*

Advantages accrue immediately after *NOIR* is stood up, whether or not *NOIR* actually succeeds in its main mission of inducing insider spies to *reconcile*!

WEAKENING OF SPY-HANDLER RELATIONSHIPS

All such relationships get weakened because with *NOIR*, there is a permanent option of escape always available to newly recruited or veteran spies. Any hostile intelligence service would have to assume that at least some of its insider spies have gone bad on them and opted to *reconcile*. Even if that weren't so, they must operate as if each of their recruited American agents was teetering on the edge of compromise.

> The biggest negative reaction to the establishment of *NOIR* will come from all the hostile intelligence services of the world. Their jobs will get much harder.

Constant availability of an escape hatch will get in the way of handlers getting away with posing to their recruited agents as the sole reliable source of support, recognition, appreciation, money, etc. Handlers must always be concerned about whether their fish will slip off the hook.

Handlers will constantly seek reassurance that their agents are still on the hook and would have to constantly work against *NOIR*. They will tend to become pushy, demand other reassurances, all of which will counter the atmosphere of warmth and friendship they have worked so hard to cultivate. This will have the opposite effect of pushing their American agents further away. Over time, *NOIR*, merely by existing, works to contaminate, undermine, and degrade all spy-handler relationships.

Handlers have another worry. They must also constantly be on guard, even when a case seems to be running smoothly, whether their recruited agents have been doubled. For all these reasons, the mere existence of *NOIR* will negatively alter the interpersonal dynamics between all insider spies and their foreign handlers.

The biggest negative reaction to the establishment of *NOIR* will come from all the hostile intelligence services of the world. Their jobs will get much harder.

ROLLING UP SPY NETWORKS BECOMES MORE LIKELY

NOIR's *reconciliation* puts pressure on still-hidden insider spies. There would be a kind of snowball effect, because each of them will now have more reason to fear that they may get unmasked. As each new insider spy steps forward to *reconcile*, more information not previously known gets disclosed. Thus, more chances that counterintelligence teams will roll up more spies and spy networks. This knowledge would work on the minds of still-hidden insider spies, weakening their resolve to stay hidden.

With every *reconciled* spy there would be a strategic dividend. With *NOIR*, identification of insider spies would no longer be dependent on random or lucky events – it would start to occur more frequently.

NOIR PROMOTES EVENTUAL READINESS TO RECONCILE

NOIR will bring to all spies mindfulness of their impossible life situations. This effect may not be immediate, because a spy may just not be ready yet for *reconciliation*. However, the mere existence of *NOIR* can plant the first seeds of doubt – and hope – for later consideration. *NOIR* can influence the spy's thinking, channeling it to interpret their life condition as it really is: stuck, trapped, and constantly worried about when the other shoe will drop. This will foster readiness to *reconcile*.

INSIDER SPY PRODUCTIVITY DECREASES IN ANTICIPATION

From the moment insider spies consider *reconciliation*, it will change their behavior. They may start to reduce cooperation with their handlers and dial down their productivity. During this deliberation phase, insider spies will turn over fewer intelligence assets.

MORALE IMPROVEMENT FOR INTELLIGENCE COMMUNITY AGENCIES

Intelligence agencies fail to detect insider spies for years. Eventually, when the news of a disclosed spy explodes in screaming headlines, the victimized agencies come to be thought of as incompetent and suffer embarrassment, ridicule and diminished reputation. This has negative internal effects on the agency workforce. With *NOIR*, these public revelations are headed off. Defections are necessarily handled quietly, behind closed doors, preventing unwelcome public reaction. Oversight authorities will have to know, but this will remain classified. An added bonus: no inspiration for copycat crimes.

PREDOMINATION: THE KEY STRATEGIC BENEFIT OF *NOIR*

NOIR shifts the international balance of espionage operations in favor of the United States, giving us a global strategic competitive advantage.

Historically, the United States has not enjoyed a robust advantage vis-à-vis other intelligence services in human intelligence (HUMINT). We have compensated for this shortfall by superiority in technical intelligence. *NOIR* helps to level the HUMINT playing field by making our intelligence community, as compared to other nations, more impenetrable.

Standing up a *NOIR* capability is culturally congruent for the United States.

The only countries that can match our capacity to credibly stand up an *NOIR* happen to be our allies, the democracies that value individuals and that share our culture: our "Cousins," such as the United Kingdom, Australia, Canada, etc. Our adversaries around the world cannot possibly compete. *NOIR* requires a culture that is humane, trustworthy, innovative, credible, reliable, and open to forgiveness, second chances and comebacks. While not perfect in these respects, the United States is uniquely situated because our national culture makes a *NOIR* workable.

By comparison, it's hard to imagine that our opponents around the world—Russia, China, Iran, North Korea, and others—could culturally pull off a *NOIR*. Nations that are totalitarian, harsh, punitive, untrust-

worthy, unreliable, or corrupt will not be able to stand up a credible *NOIR* capability. Their own citizens simply wouldn't trust them. Trust is the critical factor without which a *NOIR* cannot operate successfully. Simply put: We can do it; they can't.

Other factors that give us an advantage: The United States is geographically a big country to hide in, which is useful for concealing *reconciled* insider spies. Psychologically, we are an island nation. Americans love living here and can't imagine living anywhere else. Promises by handlers of refuge in Russia, Iran, or North Korea would not be terribly attractive to an American insider spy. Even under the reduced circumstances of a *reconciliation* agreement, spies would rather live here in the United States. *NOIR* is a mechanism only the United States and our closest allies can stand up.

ANCILLARY BENEFITS OF NOIR

1: PARTIALLY SOLVING THE PROBLEM OF THE NON-PROSECUTABLE SPY

Numerous cases of persons highly suspected of being spies are never prosecuted for want of evidence that will stand up in court. Despite case files filled to the brim with almost conclusive proof of spying, the evidence does not quite meet the threshold for charging these suspects with espionage. To quote one professional: "Most cases die in the file because we don't have a prosecutable case." Meanwhile, full surveillance is undertaken in the hope of catching suspects in the act. Once suspects notice they're under scrutiny, they get more vigilant, and then go dormant. Now what? This is very frustrating for security and counterintelligence professionals.

Given current policy, spies choose non-cooperation. Punishments for espionage are so onerous that conflicted spies find it preferable to play the game out and admit nothing.

What to do? Only half-measures are possible, which at least limit further damages. Suspects can have their accesses reduced and they can be harassed. Hardly satisfying. Finally, they can be fired on some grounds and be harassed some more (viz., the Felix Bloch case). With non-prosecutable spies, it's messy: disturbingly inconclusive, lacks the satisfaction of bringing these cases to trial, and places gaining critical Damage Assessments out of reach.

With *NOIR* in place, there would be new options. Insider spies who know they are under strong suspicion, *but do not know that they are non-prosecutable*, may on their own initiative decide to put an end to their uncertainty by turning themselves in. With *NOIR*, the balance shifts strongly to their availing themselves of *NOIR* protections.

Counterintelligence professionals can deliberately nudge suspected but non-prosecutable spies in the *NOIR* direction through hints. Better a *reconciled* spy than a non-prosecutable spy. Now, at least there would be a chance to gain the many advantages of debriefing the *reconciled* spy and getting a full Damage Assessment. As a bonus, we can "PNG" the spy's handler from the United States, thus disrupting that hostile intelligence service's recruitment operations against us.

2: GETTING TRACTION WITH IDEOLOGICAL, ETHNIC, RELIGIOUS, OR PSYCHOPATHIC SPIES

These three categories of insider spy are the hard cases. Their motivations are more deeply rooted, making them more difficult to thwart. Even so, if *NOIR* were in place, there would be points of leverage that could work.

■ IDEOLOGICAL SPIES

Time changes the outlook of all people, including ideological spies. Youthful passions cool over time. With maturity, black and white thinking fades to shades of gray. From the clearer perspective of one or two decades later, any ideology can be appreciated as too rigid and out of touch with reality. Passions for an ideology that once ran hot now become like old, cold potatoes.

Added to that are family concerns. The insider spy worries that if he gets caught, his grown children will find his original ideological motives merely ridiculous. These changes can soften even ideological spies and make them ripe targets for *NOIR*.

■ ETHNIC AND RELIGIOUS SPIES

These are harder cases because ethnic spies' motivations differ from the more typical insider spies whose motives are personal and idiosyncratic. Foreign intelligence officers who recruit by playing the ethnic card appeal to loyalties that have tribal power. Even so, candidates for this kind of recruitment are also subject to all the stresses highlighted in the earlier of the Ten Stages; they don't succumb for the sole reason of ethnic solidarity.

As with ideological spies, time shifts the inner calcu-lations of even ethnic and religious spies to weaken their affiliation with their old country or faith. Many foreign cultures strongly emphasize family integrity, duties and obligations, and respect for elders. Protecting the family from dishonor and shame is highly valued. What will happen if they get caught and their spy story leaks out? How will it affect their children who are Americanized? As heads of their families, they would feel even more like failures if their children were harmed by embar-rassment, shame, and other negative treatment.

With *NOIR* in place, even ethnic or religious spies would eventually become potential candidates for *rec-onciliation*.

■ PSYCHOPATHIC SPIES

Psychopathy can be defined as the absence of a capacity for guilt, accompanied by minimal empathy for other people. Psychopaths see other people as two-dimensional cutouts, to be used, manipulated and exploited, like pawns on a chessboard. They are expert at reading other people to take advantage of vulnera-bilities. They are like wily reptilian predators. They are upset only by the prospect of being caught or punished. If that happens, they may appear to be unhappy, sad and depressed, but only because they have been thwarted, not because of inner self-condemnation or guilt.

Psychopathy is often used as a key descriptor for insider spies. However, that may be an overused expla-nation. It's not all wrong, just incomplete as an explana-tion, as explained in Part One. Intelligence professionals at the higher levels of the pyramid of the intelligence community are less likely to be constituted that way. Many years of motivated hard work and demanding schooling, which is required to qualify for these higher positions, tends to select out psychopathic candidates. Because of less selectivity, there may be more psycho-pathic types at lower levels of the pyramid.

Psychopathic spies, because they lack strong morals and are self-absorbed and exploitative, may appear to be much harder for *NOIR* to manage. Surprisingly, that may not be true. Who knows better than a psychopath which side of the bread is buttered? *NOIR* does not require the spy to possess a conscience!

Psychopaths may avail themselves of *NOIR* not for reasons of guilt, but just to save their skins. *Reconciliation* for them would mainly be for their own convenience, and out of the fear of being accidentally betrayed. Psychopaths will make their decisions based purely on calculating what works to optimize their self-interest.

So what? From a counterintelligence point of view, the net outcome is still better. The spying stops, the spy spills out useful information during the Damage Assessment, and he is neutralized as a continuing security threat. If he had not taken advantage of *NOIR*, he might never have been identified or caught so soon. Or, if identified, he might have been non-prosecutable (see previous), and unwilling to divulge his knowledge.

3: MANAGING DIFFICULT "GRAY ZONE" PERSONNEL PROBLEMS

NOIR provides a mechanism for managing difficult "gray zone" problems, incidents just below the threshold for terminating intelligence officer careers.

For example, when our own intelligence officers come close to crossing certain lines – not necessarily into spying – but into zones where questionable decisions and judgments weaken the integrity of operations. When such incidents are not reported, it creates the problem. To report them may risk serious career setbacks, and for the lack of a safer way to report these matters, our intelligence strength suffers. With *NOIR* in place, with safer-to-use reporting mechanisms, some of these matters could be better managed. Two examples follow:

■ BEING PITCHED BY AN ADVERSARIAL INTELLIGENCE SERVICE

Being pitched and not reporting it because of worries it could negatively affect career. The intelligence officer may fear it would be interpreted by management that he is broadcasting signals of vulnerability, so he prefers to never mention it. Or, an intelligence officer may simply not want to have to leave the country where he's serving, so he stays silent. In both cases, the details of what happened would be useful to know

■ CROSSING ROMANTIC BOUNDARY LINES

An intelligence officer may cross the line romantically with a recruited agent, or with another intelligence officer, adversary or ally, and for obvious reasons, not report it. No need to explain why this can be a problem. A safer reporting mechanism would serve all parties better.

4: PROVIDING AN EMPLOYEE ASSISTANCE PROGRAM (EAP) OF LAST RESORT

Fair or not, EAPs inside intelligence community agencies are not well trusted. EAPs are suspected of divulging personal problems to agency management

or security offices. Unfortunately, sometimes there are grounds for these concerns. This gives an excuse for many who could really benefit from getting help, especially men. Male pride and ego, with tendencies to deny and delay, offer excuses for men to avoid getting help from internal EAPs.

Most of the time internal EAPs can serve their clients well. Agency personnel may self-refer for services, and management, or even fellow employees, can urge their colleagues to get help. Personnel with serious problems showing overt disturbing behaviors may become so obvious that management will simply demand that they check in with EAP, and then good things can happen. These case categories are not the big concerns.

For counterintelligence purposes, the real worries are the cases of personnel who feel desperate and overwhelmed by the *Psychological Perfect Storms* referred to in Part One. Some can endure these storms but somehow retain the ability to conceal outward signs of distress. These are the true worries. They can invisibly snap into a *Personal Bubble Psychology*, marked by massively distorted thinking, resulting in bad decisions, like crossing over into spying.

Distrust of internal EAPs is the key problem. If an external EAP were made available as a last resort option for help, a certain number of these hardcore cases might take advantage of it to get help – knowing that they would not necessarily be immediately reported to their home agency's management. *NOIR* would be the perfect entity to house this functionality. This will be discussed in more detail in Section B, which addresses Prevention.

5: SMOOTHING THE OUTPLACEMENT PROCESS FOR WHEN ALL ELSE FAILS

What to do about "hot potato" employees? These are the ones who can't seem to stay within reasonable boundaries of behavior. They are "loose cannons," who may be quite brilliant, but whose judgment doesn't match up. They are unstable, unpredictable; at times very effective, at other times placing themselves or their home agencies at major risk of causing embarrassing operational failures or worse. After countless efforts to straighten them out, managers may lose hope and finally, out of need to protect important equities, conclude such persons have to go.

How can this be accomplished safely?

If pressed too hard, these unstable persons can get pushed over the edge, react with bitter fury, and become even bigger problems than before – to include the risk of turning to espionage. On the other hand, not doing anything to clip their wings may give mixed messages of tolerance, adding the risk that they will cause further damage. It's a no-win situation for managers. In the private sector, a whole new niche industry has evolved to help deal with this: outplacement.

Here's how it works: First, the problem employee meets with a manager who delivers the hard news – he is being fired. No long story is presented about why. Just a firm: "It's not working out." Then the employee is told: "But we want you to transition into another position where you fit better and you can succeed. We've engaged another company that is expert in helping people like you to make a smooth transition, and that company's representative is waiting right now to be introduced to you."

Immediately, the employee is escorted into another office and introduced to the outplacement professional, who takes over. The former manager quietly leaves. This outplacement professional is calm, friendly and respectful. The newly fired employee gets a chance to vent his shock, hurt, anger and his other intense emotions to this new, caring, sympathetic and supportive person who is not an employee of the firing company. This allows for a graceful, soft landing, and a diversion of attention away from the firing company to the new supportive entity.

The next meeting takes place off-premises, in the offices of the outplacement firm. There, more support is offered to the fired employee, and more opportunity for venting. Also, he is given daily access to a well-appointed office, where he can explore new job options. The key idea is to cushion sensitive feelings, restore dignity, and rebuild confidence.

As an office external to any of the intelligence community agencies, *NOIR* can be used for outplacement. *NOIR* can choreograph the exiting of unstable or difficult employees who would be permitted to bow out gracefully, avoiding unwelcome trouble. Costs would be tiny compared to undoing the costs of espionage.

SECTION B:
PREVENTING SPYING

Preventing spying is the third key Strategic benefit of *NOIR*, achieved by way of two approaches: raising the barriers for crossing the line, and lowering the pressures for crossing the line.

RAISING THE BARRIERS FOR CROSSING THE LINE

CORE IDEA: REDEFINING THE MEANING OF SPYING

In Part One, a deeper understanding was developed about the root causes of what leads to insider spying. In Section A of this paper, which addresses stopping spying, it was asserted that focusing on the root causes of spying, what goes on in Stages One through Three, surprisingly doesn't matter that much because of the phenomenon of convergence. But it was promised that this knowledge is not useless. Now, here in Section B, which addresses preventing spying, that knowledge becomes very useful.

As for root causes, rather than the usual explanations trotted out about MICE (money, ideology, compromise and ego) or other notions, Part One asserts that it has much more to do with *an intolerable sense of personal failure as privately defined by that person.* This can occur when enormous stresses build up on a prospective spy, culminating in a *Psychological Perfect Storm*, which totally overwhelms him, making him feel like he's drowning. There's nothing to be proud of here – this loss of control over navigating his life. Nearly all insider spies are male. The Storm engenders a sense of personal incompetence, defeat, and panic, demolishing everything the prospective spy needs to sustain his male pride and ego.

Intelligence community and law enforcement professionals, and the general public, regard an insider spy as being despicable, a greedy malcontent, a malicious villain, an evil outlaw, a traitor-bastard (not entirely wrong on all counts). This stands in contrast to something hidden in plain sight within our wider culture: Perversely, for a spy to be all these horrible things is not all bad.

Think of all the attention. We know how intensely curious everyone seems to be about what makes insider spies tick. Books are written, movies are produced.

More to the point, to be a defiant outlaw, villain, or evil genius, attracts a peculiar fascination and respect. For example, consider the catch phrase from the street: "I'm bad!" Which really means, "I'm good!" Badness gets converted to being a positive by salvaging someone's reputation when he has "nothing left to lose." Capturing this perverse pride: "If I go down, I'm going down in flames!"

We can understand that this is actually a psychological defensive maneuver to conceal the truth: The insider spy did not choose his bad path because he's some kind of dark hero. He fell into spying because he could not deal with the difficult knowledge that he's been proven to be, by his own measure, a Loser/Failure.

Being a loser and a failure in our culture, and in most other cultures, is just not cool. It's merely sad and pathetic. It has an odor. It's cause for pity, not scorn.

Now, picture that this deeper, more correct truth gets drilled into the public's mind with force and energy. Imagine that these messages get pushed into our culture, not only within the intelligence community, but also into the wider world of our national life and conversation. To use the currently fashionable language, it would be changing the narrative, shifting the paradigm. *NOIR* proposes to proactively redefine the shared meaning of spying this way: if someone descends into insider spying, he is openly declaring to himself – and to the whole world, when he gets caught – that he is a Loser/Failure.

This redefinition takes away the dark attraction that to spy is glamorous, romantic, or confers a cool, bad-boy notoriety. No, spying is not cool. It's odd. Being Bad may be oddly attractive – but being not cool is certainly unattractively odd. There's absolutely no attraction to being a Loser/Failure.

Spying is NOT cool.

The plan would be to engineer a cultural shift to this new, more correct, shared meaning. The tone must be right: not angry, mean or accusative, but rather concerned, sad and disappointed. Shifting a shared meaning is not something that can be achieved instantly. It would require a deliberate, consistent and frequently communicated message over about three years that hammers home the point. Advertising and public relations professionals are experts at devising and executing such campaigns. There are many examples of successful campaigns of this type, from campaigns to stop smoking, to not mix drinking and driving, to getting proud Texans to quit littering their highways: "Don't mess with Texas."[6]

Once the public perception is transformed to accept this redefinition, then effectively, it becomes so. Thereafter, anyone contemplating the decision to spy must take into account how everyone else will view this act. Spying begins to lose its allure. The decision to spy becomes equivalent to becoming the most uncool person in high school – something to be avoided at all costs.

As the shared meaning of spying shifts from Bad/Outlaw to Loser/Failure, it starts to exert a profound protective constraint on anyone in danger of slipping over the edge. It won't magically undo the desperation, panic and terror of someone drowning in dire straits. But it will strengthen the last residue of their male pride, ego and dignity, to help them resist crossing the line.

Imagine the inner debate of someone struggling to stay sane and afloat in the midst of a *Psychological Perfect Storm*: "Things are terribly bad for me. I don't think I can make it. But…I'm not a Loser. I'm NOT a Failure! Things are very bad for me right now – but I can handle it. I will handle it! Spy? I thought of that. No way! I'm not a Loser/Failure! I have to figure out some other way to manage things."

LOWERING THE PRESSURES FOR CROSSING THE LINE

To prevent spying, we need measures designed to help a person climb back when they're in danger of getting overwhelmed by the stresses that are battering them. To deliver these rescuing measures requires that *NOIR* expand its offerings beyond its core functionality of *reconciliation*.

Reconciliation can work because of two key factors associated with *NOIR*: its new and unique package of protections; its existence separate and apart from all the other agencies of the intelligence community. For an insider spy, or for someone at risk for becoming one, it is no small thing to be able to access a resource at a far remove from their home agency. As an office external to their home agency, *NOIR*, with its separation and distance, creates in and of itself a welcoming tone of safety, security, and hope.

NOIR can add two key functionalities: an Employee Assistance Program (EAP) of Last Resort, and an Outplacement capability. These functionalities, already discussed, can serve as pressure-relieving valves to reduce the typical life pressures that push people beyond their coping strengths into contemplating drastic options, like insider spying. In Section C, some further details will be presented about these resources.

In listing the Ancillary Benefits of *NOIR* previously, the availability of an enhanced suite of resources, now under discussion, was intended as a way to help manage difficult problems, thereby heading off dangerous situations that could lead to insider spying. Among others, these are: the Non-Prosecutable Spy, and the "Gray Zone" Personnel Problems, including failure to report getting pitched, romantic indiscretions, etc.

SECTION C:
NOIR: THE PROPOSED NEW GOVERNMENT ENTITY

FOUR MAIN CHARACTERISTICS OF NOIR

1: SMALL

NOIR is designed to fulfill a limited role for all the other intelligence agencies. Not aspiring to be a Three Letter Agency, NOIR can work to enhance the success of the entire intelligence community.

2: INDEPENDENT AND SEPARATE FROM ALL INTELLIGENCE COMMUNITY AGENCIES

The separation and independence of NOIR turns out to be one of its most powerful attributes because it's safe, secure, and not contaminated by the spillover of negative feelings that are associated with their home agency. Unfortunately, in many cases, anger, bitterness, and distrust directed at the home agency, prevents stressed employees from availing themselves of helping resources internal to their home agency. The resources, while there in name, in reality serve more as a fig leaf than as a true resource for the most difficult problems. Independent NOIR can provide the cure for this shortcoming.

3: INEXPENSIVE

Not another intelligence agency! During this age of budget constraints, this is an understandable concern. NOIR will be designed to be cheap to operate, just a rounding error in intelligence budgets. Best to think of it as an insurance premium for a very expensive enterprise. It's a way to lay off risk. The expense to the nation of just one major insider spy is almost incalculable. Saving those losses would offset the cost of NOIR for decades of its operation. "Pay me now or pay me later."

■ STAFFING

Staffing would be very limited, comprising almost no full-time staff for the core *reconciliation* function. Staff would be recruited from the ranks of retired counter-intelligence professionals, seasoned, savvy individuals, who would be invited to join, as in an elite military unit; only the best of the best.

These retired intelligence officers would be proud to be selected and would be happy to participate just to stay in the game. Just for the honor of it, they would likely serve as Dollar-A-Year men and women. They would be older; therefore they would project a more authoritative and parental image, which would instill a greater sense of security in the *reconciling* spy.

Given their age and life wisdom, they are likely to be more philosophical and less passionate in their attitudes, and therefore, they would be less likely to unleash unbridled reflexive anger towards the *reconciling* spy. Also, they would harbor less rigid loyalty and attachment to their original home agency. They would be able to liaise well with their original home agency since they would still have contacts there.

This would be a part-time staff, called upon as needed, more like a volunteer fire department; otherwise, dormant, except for training and occasional meetings.

Reconciling spies would be matched with staff from a different home agency, precisely to avoid negative emotional complications from both sides. A case manager approach would be used. NOIR would seek to match a good fit that works for the *reconciling* spy. The case manager will become the *reconciled* spy's confidante, friend, advisor, advocate, protector, and guide. He will treat the spy with respect to preserve dignity.

He will also step into the role of the spy's former handler, but with a different mission: to elicit as much as possible of use to our intelligence community; to maximally assess damage; to discover clues to identify other spies and spy networks; and to prime the *reconciled* spy for possible doubling, if feasible. This multiplicity of roles will call for the highest level of professionalism.

■ PHYSICAL LOCATIONS

No fancy brick and mortar venues. That wouldn't work anyhow, as safe houses would have to be the primary locations for all *reconciliation* activities. Some of the other NOIR functions would require modest office locations, such as EAP and Outplacement. Some of these could be co-located at one of the other intelligence agencies without harm, though others obviously would need separate locations.

CERTAIN OTHER FUNCTIONS AND THEIR COSTS

Some things can be contracted to existing agencies. For example, some *reconciled* spies would have to adopt new identities and perhaps this function could be out-sourced to WITSEC. Why reinvent the wheel? Other functions will need more budget. As described below, some components of *NOIR*, such as EAP and Outplacement would have typical staffing and administrative costs, which could be kept limited.

4: SECRECY REGARDING NOIR IS NOT DESIRABLE

Secrecy about the existence of *NOIR*, though it's very much a part of the intelligence community, perhaps surprisingly, is not desirable for the most part. Secrecy would actively work against *NOIR*.

A top goal of *NOIR* would be to get its message out about the availability of *reconciliation* to everyone in the entire intelligence community. To make everyone aware of this option is important since singling out any specific individuals or subgroups would be counterproductive. The net must be cast widely, as an equal opportunity offering. Global awareness of the *NOIR* suite of resources, which are external to home agencies, gives them their power of rescue.

Must the existence and details of *NOIR* be hidden from the general public, and most of all, hostile foreign intelligence services? No. Why bother? They will find out anyhow. Their knowledge of it does not get in the way of its successful operation.[7]

On the other hand, the mechanics of *reconciliation* must remain in the black for it to work at all. What happens after contact is established with a newly *reconciling* insider spy must of course, remain secret, and that would also hold true for certain of the other *NOIR* measures previously described.

COMPONENTS OF NOIR

THE MISSION OF STOPPING SPYING

■ RECONCILIATION BRANCH

This branch would execute the most unique and sensitive functionality of *NOIR*. Getting the word out about this option would be the job of a different branch. Making *reconciliation* work with real insider spies is this branch's responsibility.

The first and most delicate stage would be establishing secure and safe contact with a candidate for *reconciliation*. Think of how scared the prospect would be. He would literally be placing his life in the hands of an entity and process that he would not be sure he could trust. Communications would have to be secure in both directions. The tradecraft details of this early stage will have to be worked out by experienced intelligence professionals.

The dance of initial contact, the negotiation of the terms of surrender, the first in-person meetings, the assignment of the intake officer who will act as the case manager, the development of a good working relationship, the inclusion of a Damage Assessment team (that must learn new practices to conduct the process quietly), liaising with the home agency's internal counterintelligence component, and the FBI's National Security team, the evaluation for suitability for double agent operations, and so forth, all of these would have to be choreographed and managed in a clandestine manner.

Moving the insider spy outside of his home agency would have to be accomplished. Various reasons can be used: a promotion elsewhere; a secret operation elsewhere; a transfer to another agency on detail; an inheritance; illness; a family situation; an early retirement, etc.

THE MISSION OF PREVENTING SPYING

■ PUBLIC AFFAIRS AND OUTREACH BRANCH

The job of this branch is to promote *NOIR* and educate publics inside and outside the intelligence community. Within the intelligence community, training weeks would be scheduled semi-annually, mandatory for all personnel. This could be accomplished online at workplace computers and would last only about an hour. Video dramatizations would be aired that depict various pressured life situations, how they can pile up on an individual, and how to survive them. Messaging with guidance, remedies, resources that can be tapped for help, would be interspersed between these interesting dramatic episodes.

The *NOIR* suite of resources, including *reconciliation* would be prominently featured. A short test would end each session. Thus, everyone would be educated about what spying really means, and what to do to escape if currently ensnared. True-to-life outcomes of spies would be recounted to puncture the romance of it. The tone taken would avoid the usual hard-edged warnings and threats, but rather would take a straightforward tone, reserved, concerned. Occasionally, large group events may be useful. Of course, virtually all of this is preaching to the choir, but could be of immense interest to vulnerable individuals, and to those who have already crossed the line.

■ RESEARCH BRANCH

This branch would specialize in studying spy psychology to deepen the knowledge. It would seek to establish best practices and lessons learned. There would be studies focusing on continuous improvement of *reconciliation* practices, on the subject of human failure, and so forth.

Incarcerated spies are an untapped precious national resource. It might be very useful to gather them together in a special facility in the Washington, DC area, instead of dispersing them throughout the federal prison population, so that more research can be undertaken to understand them better.

The true problem of spying resides in the hearts and minds of the spies themselves. Unfortunately, current national policy regarding incarcerated spies gets in the way. Initially, during the extensive debriefings that follow arrest, aggressive efforts are made to study spies. However, it stays superficial. Understandably, the tone of these debriefings is hostile, adversarial, and intrusive. This approach destroys the chance to truly get to know the spy. Understanding them on a deeper level will be the key to devising better protective measures. Sun Tzu wisely advised: "Keep your friends close and your enemies closer."

■ EMPLOYEE ASSISTANCE PROGRAM (OF LAST RESORT) BRANCH

This branch would operate as previously described, also using a case manager approach. To keep this functionality within budget, it would be best to recruit top quality, cleared practitioners in the fields of mental health, finance, business, law, etc., who could see the referrals in their own offices and report back and coordinate with *NOIR*'s central office. Budget should be allocated to pay for these services, at least initially.

Remember: these cases are the "hot potatoes." Costs to pull them back from the brink would be a very small compared to repairing the damages if the worst happens. Anything that reduces stress and anxiety would be smart to do, and should be done with minimal bureaucratic interference. That includes easy loans to bail out those in a deep financial hole. It's a tradeoff. Wouldn't we rather have someone in a position of trust get shielded from disaster before they melt down?

■ OUTPLACEMENT BRANCH

Judge William Webster (former Director of both FBI and CIA), in comments to me, suggested the idea for this branch.[8] Judge Webster mused that one of his biggest problems was dealing with personnel characterized in this paper as "hot potatoes." Unfortunately, a percentage of these are not salvageable. Then what? The problem is how to exit them gracefully, without pushing them over the edge. The goal would be to avoid public dramas, so that for the problematic individual and his home agency, there will be a "soft landing."

■ GENERAL ADMINISTRATIVE BRANCH

This branch would house the usual functions that any organization requires. However, there would be a few functions that would be uniquely necessary for *NOIR*.

Security would be especially critical. *NOIR* would become a top target for all sophisticated hostile foreign intelligence services because they would be desperate to know if one of their valued American agents turned on them and *reconciled*. Therefore, *NOIR* might require even more stringent security measures to protect that information. While many of *NOIR*'s functions would be in the public eye by design, the inner workings of *reconciliation* must be thoroughly concealed. There would be a need for upgraded legal support because of the complexity of *reconciliation* cases. Negotiating or terminating *NOIR* protections, managing liaison relationships, with other intelligence agencies, with congressional oversight committees, with the White House, with the courts, would be very demanding.

CONCLUSIONS

DEFINING SUCCESS

NOIR becomes the first counterintelligence program that is fully accountable.

With conventional counterintelligence practice, we can never know if the job of ferreting out every last insider spy is fully accomplished. How to prove a negative? As they say: "Absence of evidence is not evidence of absence." By contrast, with *NOIR*, results are positive and measurable: Count the number of insider spies who choose to *reconcile*. *NOIR* is a testable hypothesis: Either it works or it doesn't work. After a fair trial period, say five years, if absolutely no insider spies present themselves for *reconciliation*, it would clearly be proven a failed idea.

There should be a "sunset provision," so that if *NOIR* proves unsuccessful, it would be shut down.

To carry this further, *NOIR* may begin to illuminate one disturbing unknown: Just how many insider spies are there? We really have no way to know. A case could be made that the numbers of which we are aware (about 150 prosecutions since the end of World War II), give no clue as to the true numbers. Remember the non-prosecutable spies that never end up in a courtroom – how do we numerically account for them? If *NOIR* flushes out a certain number of previously unidentified insider spies, while this wouldn't provide a full answer, it could begin to paint a more realistic picture of the size of the problem.

NOIR must report its statistics to appropriate authorities both at the uppermost levels of the intelligence community, as well as to Congressional oversight committees. Reports would include numbers of employees who chose to *reconcile*, and also the level of their seriousness. Some *reconcilers* would be of modest importance, but others would be of great importance, at the level of an Ames or Hanssen, so establishing categories would be helpful. The first cases seeking *reconciliation* might be the "small fry," or old spies from many years in the past. It might take a while before the more serious current cases start to emerge, only after they feel more secure that *NOIR* is working as advertised.

Another indicator of usefulness would be utilization of the other functionalities that *NOIR* would offer, such as EAP and Outplacement.

A cost benefit analysis could be devised. One concept would be the "Value of an Insider Spy Case," to compare against the operating costs of *NOIR*. The "value" of any case could be calculated based on the potential losses listed in the discussion of the Economic Analysis of the Cost of A Spy. Each *reconciled* spy could be analyzed to determine in detail the savings achieved by interrupting his career. Just as examples: One estimate of the financial costs of the Ronald Pelton/Ivy Bells case was in the range of $3 billion in 1980s dollars; a recent estimate of Robert Hanssen's tab: $20 billion. As the savings accumulate, spy after spy, total savings could be viewed as offsetting the costs of operating *NOIR*. How to value the soft costs of a case, related to protecting agency morale and reputation, etc., would be harder to calculate.

IMPLEMENTING *NOIR*: THE NEXT STEPS

Standing up *NOIR* will not be an easy task. There will be enormous hurdles to overcome, based on opposition by various intelligence agencies with reality-based, practical grounds for concern, or concerns related to turf; by Congressional and other political stakeholders; by adverse expressions coming from the public, etc. There will have to be vigilance that *NOIR* gets set up properly and not designed with flaws that result in a programmed failure.

Further discussion is warranted of the many issues and difficulties that are valid to consider before adopting *NOIR*. That said, if our national security gets vitally enhanced, all the challenges would be very worth overcoming. *NOIR* could be an exciting, novel, innovative breakthrough to advance progress in managing the vexing problem of insider spies.

■ ■ ■

I am very interested in your thoughts, comments, suggestions, ideas, etc., about this White Paper. You can provide your feedback on our website: **www. NOIR4USA.org**. —*David L. Charney, MD*

"Keep your friends close
and your enemies closer."
—SunTzu

"Always give your enemy an exit."
—SunTzu

ENDNOTES

1 "True Psychology of the Insider Spy"

Published in the journal of the Association of Former Intelligence Officers (AFIO), The Intelligencer, (2010). This paper is Part One of the two-part White Paper, and is available as a pdf on the our website: NOIR4USA.org, and also on the website of the Office of the National Counterintelligence Executive (ONCIX), under "Top CI Issues/Insider Threats" at NCIX.gov.

2 & 4 The Terms: Reconciliation and *NOIR*

Reconciliation was the first term considered, since it seemed a perfect word to describe the proposed process whereby an insider spy voluntarily turns himself in. Various existing uses, listed below, already captured the flavor of such a process:

- Marital counseling – bringing couples far apart back together;
- Bookkeeping and accounting – *reconciling* books and accounts so they add up properly;
- Congressional bills – many of which contain the word *reconciliation* in their names, indicating final compromise on the law after it was negotiated between the two houses;
- Truth and *Reconciliation* – the process in South Africa following the remarkable peaceful end to apartheid. Nelson Mandela wisely pushed for full disclosure of all the bad stories of the past regime as a foundation for forgiveness and moving on;
- Sacrament of Confession has been given this new term, *Reconciliation*, within the Catholic Church, implying a more forgiving attitude in the context of coming back to God after a long separation.

NOIR came to mind after the term *reconciliation* was settled upon. To come up with a name that lent itself to a good acronym, the letter R, of course, had to be utilized. To avoid any presumption about a Three Letter Agency, four letters would be necessary for the acronym. The obvious choice became *NOIR*. This helped to devise the name of the new government entity proposed to implement *reconciliation*: the National Office for Intelligence Reconciliation.

The acronym *NOIR* carries a flavor of the world of spying because of noir movies and style. It means black in French. And of course, there are all the black programs and budgets that exist in the world of intelligence, so that's a natural fit. But there are other references to black as a term historically associated with intelligence, including the American Black Chamber in the State Department of the 1920s, headed by Herbert Yardley, the first government organization devoted to cryptanalysis; Cardinal Richelieu's Cabinet Noir in France, and so forth.

3 "Sharks in a Shark Tank"

This is described in Part One, "True Psychology of the Insider Spy." Sharks can swim nicely together but if one of them gets nicked and starts to bleed, all the others will instantly turn to attack, predators going after prey. This explains what happens when someone attempts to "do the right thing" and turns himself in to his home agency's office of security. No warm welcomes, just ferocious treatment, like prey.

5 American works of literature about disloyal citizens who want to come back

- *The Man Without A Country*

From Wikipedia: "This is a short story by American writer Edward Everett Hale, first published in The Atlantic in December 1863...It is the story of American Army lieutenant Philip Nolan, who renounces his country during a trial for treason and is consequently sentenced to spend the rest of his days at sea without so much as a word of news about the United States." It describes his repentance and desperate wish to hear about and see his beloved country again.

- *The Devil and Daniel Webster*

From Wikipedia: "This is a short story by Stephen Vincent Benét. This retelling of the classic German Faust tale is based on the short story "The Devil and Tom Walker," written by Washington Irving. Benét's version of the story centers on a New Hampshire farmer who sells his soul to the Devil and is defended by Daniel Webster, a fictional version of the famous lawyer and orator." Again, an American gone astray, who needs to be defended by the very best lawyer, to try to get off the hook and come back.

6 "Don't Mess With Texas"

Frank Luntz described the story of this campaign, its conception, rollout and success, in *Words That Work*, 2007. More on this in Wikipedia: http://en.wikipedia.org/wiki/Don't_Mess_with_Texas, and in the "Don't Mess With Texas" website: dontmesswithtexas.org

7 What can hostile foreign intelligence services do to defeat *NOIR*?

In the lead up to *NOIR* getting stood up, perhaps it will come up for debate in Congress in the Select Committees. The SVR (the latest version of the old KGB) and its ilk, will not be happy and will perhaps file an amicus brief to protest that *NOIR* would give an unfair advantage to the US in the world of espionage (only kidding).

More seriously, the only card hostile intelligence services could play after *NOIR* was already stood up would be to badmouth *NOIR* as not being the safe refuge it claims to be. Hostile intelligence services would have every reason to warn their recruited American agents that if they went forward with *reconciliation*, it would backfire on them. After they would turn themselves in and get squeezed dry during their Damage Assessments, the US would turn around, claim they had somehow violated their agreements, and in the end, they anyhow would get thrown into prison. In other words, that *NOIR* was just a scam. For this reason, *NOIR* must always operate with the highest level of probity and propriety, and not too quickly declare *reconciled* spies to be violators of their agreements. Why give ammunition for this kind of attack?

Nevertheless, hostile intelligence services will make that claim. But what evidence could they come up with? How could they prove it? If *reconciliation* proceeds according to plan, the process would be invisible to the outside world. Ah, but of course, a hostile intelligence service would know that one of their agents *reconciled*, because that agent would go off the radar for them. Could they try to spoil it, take revenge on the *reconciled* spy by setting up some scheme to make it appear that the *reconciled* agent betrayed his *NOIR* agreement? Then it would be game up, and the spy would go to prison.

Next, they could point to the case with the accusation: "Look, the Americans cannot be trusted! They lured this agent in with false promises, and see how it played out!" All kinds of stratagems of this type could be tried to defeat the attraction of *NOIR*. The harder they try, however, the more implicit credence they would give to *NOIR*. Agents would wonder: "Why are they trying so hard to turn me against *NOIR*? What are they afraid of?" The harder hostile intelligence services would try, the more attractive and interesting *NOIR* would become. As they say in Hollywood, "There's no such thing as bad publicity."

Plus, recruited agents researching *NOIR* out of curiosity could read this very paper and figure out for themselves that all hostile intelligence services must be desperately trying to neutralize *NOIR* (which is why this line of discussion is included here). Mr. Spy, you read it here first!

NOIR has to take into account that sophisticated efforts will be attempted by hostile intelligence agencies to defeat it. One initiative could involve an orchestrated plot to use an agent to falsely *reconcile*, with the deliberate aim of having the process go bad — all for creating proof that *NOIR* cannot be trusted. Would hostile intelligence services waste an agent just for that purpose? Why not?

I believe (without proof), that two of the spies I worked with, both Special Agents of the FBI, were deliberately blown by SVR, and that's why they were caught. After long tenures as productive agents, eventually all insider spies get to be "worn out shoes." That's because they get to the end of their careers within their intelligence community and will shortly retire. They no longer will get to keep their accesses to classified material, so they are no longer useful. The story line that they've been sold all along is that upon retiring from their spy careers, they will now be able to enjoy the fruits of their labor, with quiet honor and appreciation from the service that ran them.

However, I believe that such old agents can have one last utility: they can be deliberately blown. For example, SVR is probably cynical and clever enough to do this as this strategy can achieve a number of useful purposes for them, if not played too often. As the ultimate chess players, SVR would view this as a pawn sacrifice, to protect a more valued piece still on the board. They would try to make it appear that the given up spy was responsible for the losses that the still hidden and valuable spy actually perpetrated.

The drama of the disclosure of a long-time spy will draw enormous attention and will distract the compromised service from noticing that a still productive and major SVR spy is still working away in the shadows. There will be consternation and turmoil in the compromised agency. It's like sticking a branch into a hornet's nest. Thus, the last utility of an old, used-up spy is to mess with the minds of the American intelligence community. It brings to mind a saying from the old-time Chicago stockyards: "We use every part of the pig except the squeal."

TWO FAIR WARNINGS:

To compromised agencies: You just had the "good luck" to identify a long-concealed insider spy who just happens to be close to retirement. While you're trying to manage the ugly aftermath of this disclosure, amidst the frenzy, and the relief of catching the spy, can somebody else be quietly busy, thankful for the distraction?

To long-time insider spies close to retirement: Pray that *NOIR* gets stood up. You may get a chance to exit in one piece – before your handler's service gets one last utility out of you.

8 "Hot Potato" Personnel Problems, and Outplacement

Judge William Webster, former FBI Director and former Director of Central Intelligence, the only person who has ever served in both high positions, brought up this area of concern to me. When I briefed him, after taking in the gist of *reconciliation* and *NOIR*, he mentioned that these proposed mechanisms might be useful for managing what were some of his most difficult problems. No claim is made here that Judge Webster supports *NOIR*, in whole or in part, but I do credit Judge Webster for suggesting this added functionality for *NOIR*.

PART THREE

PROPOSING A NEW, COMPREHENSIVE STRATEGY TO PREVENT, NOT DETECT, INSIDER THREAT IN THE INTELLIGENCE COMMUNITY (IC)

SECTION A:

THE PROBLEM: INSIDER THREAT

Recent dramatic security breaches have drawn increasing attention to the insider threat problem. These breaches have captured headlines and have featured perpetrators such as classic state-sponsored insider spies like the recent Chinese moles as well as so-called whistleblowers like Chelsea Manning and Edward Snowden.

My previous white paper, NOIR, proposed an off-ramp exit solution, which does not yet exist, for those who have crossed the line. Quoting Sun Tzu: "Always leave your enemy an exit."[1] Extending the logic, why not off-ramp exits, meaning robust prevention mechanisms, for before they cross the line?

ANALYZING FAILED LINKS IN SECURITY CHAINS

Security breaches and other insider threat events are the endpoints that indicate a failure occurred somewhere along the sequence of links in security chains. These links are the protective measures intended to counter potentially disastrous breaches. Breaches are proof that the links failed.

Failed security chains in the IC should be analyzed the same way the National Transportation Safety Board (NTSB) goes about studying aircraft disasters. The NTSB seeks to understand how each link failed in chains that resulted in disasters and whether protective links that should have been built into security chains were simply missing.

MISSING LINKS IN IC SECURITY CHAINS: OFF-RAMP EXITS

This paper asserts that there are two critical missing links in IC security chains. These missing links can be described as two types of *off-ramp exits*: exits for *before* someone crosses the line and exits for *after* someone crosses the line. The absence of these two links in IC security chains weakens effective management of IC insider threat.

If both missing links were added to the considerable number of existing and planned detection links — which at present seem to be the only game in town — a *full spectrum solution* would come into existence for the comprehensive management of insider threat.

DISCLAIMER

Drawing attention to the shortcomings of detection does not mean that detection has little value for managing insider threat. Far from it. Detection is vitally necessary as one of the two key components of the classic *good cop-bad cop* dyad, universally employed for managing criminal offenders.

Every IC employee is on notice that a full range of detection methodologies continuously operate, creating powerful deterrence to not cross the line. With exciting new technological advances on the horizon, detection will continue to strengthen our national security.

That said, acknowledging the enduring and critical importance of detection should not keep us from examining its limitations. This paper will assert that there is an overreliance on detection, not that it is unnecessary. Currently, it is mostly bad cop and very little good cop, mostly stick and very little carrot.

While this paper will highlight many of the limitations of detection, my primary intention is to counter the IC's tendency to put nearly all of its eggs into the detection basket. Hopefully, critical thinking about detection will motivate the IC to reconsider relying so exclusively on it. The thesis of this white paper is that neglect of prevention strategies leaves too much on the table, too many opportunities to more effectively manage insider threat. Containing insider threat is too important to limit our toolset. We need more tools in the arsenal.

SECTION B

SCOPE OF THE PROBLEM

IMPORTANCE OF PREVENTION DESPITE ITS NEGLECT

The IC invests immense effort and resources into collecting, analyzing, and producing finished intelligence products, so it is demoralizing when insider threat events render them either useless or they wind up being used against us.

Prevention's importance is captured by the old sayings: "An ounce of prevention is worth a pound of cure" and "a stitch in time saves nine." Prevention is the one chance to head off disastrous insider threat events before serious damages are inflicted.

Despite that, prevention routinely suffers from neglect because it is not perceived to be as important as collecting and analyzing positive intelligence, or as compelling as detecting and catching insider threat actors red-handed in the act.

It is also fair to say that prevention, as currently practiced, has not been that successful.

OVERLY FOCUSING ON DETECTION AT THE EXPENSE OF PREVENTION

Newly hired IC employees are generally very carefully vetted, and only the most skilled, motivated, and patriotic prospects survive processing for clearance. Despite these strenuous efforts, very rarely, employees who started off good can turn bad.

Insider spies are different from professional hostile foreign intelligence entity (FIE) officers who, as their main aim, have the goal of penetrating our IC to steal our secrets from the very beginning of their employment.

To detect the bad actors, the IC has aggressively pursued innovative high-technology surveillance techniques and deployed and tightened up a full range of security measures. But what about what happens first, the mystery of why good employees turn bad?

Insider threat events originate within the minds of individuals. That is where it starts. Always.

Despite knowing that, relatively little attention has been paid to developing ways to shift the thinking of potential insider threat actors *before* they choose to cross the line.

The IC's strategy has been to mostly do what the IC knows how to do best – detection – not what is more needed to be done.

Prevention remains the weakest link in the IC security chain.

GREAT HOPES OF THE MOMENT

Great hopes have accompanied the rise of artificial intelligence (AI), big data, algorithms, and machine learning (ML), the bright shiny objects of the moment. There is a shared assumption that these high-tech innovations will introduce all that is necessary to finally resolve the challenging problem of insider threat.

DIRTY LITTLE SECRET OF COUNTERINTELLIGENCE (CI)

Detection, for the attention it gets, has almost never caught any major spies. Nevertheless, somehow insider spies do get caught. How does it usually happen?

Nearly all major spy cases have been solved when someone from within the other side's intelligence service (i.e., the KGB) decided to cross over to our side, bearing *gifts*. To prove their *bona fides*, they brought over the names of IC employees their service were handling or enough key information that pointed to these traitors in our midst. As a result, some major spies eventually do get caught. However, the way they get caught is why detection cannot claim that much of the credit.

Giving credit where it is due, once insider spies do get identified as described, the FBI, in cooperation with other IC counterintelligence and security components, is quite effective doing what is necessary to close cases and get the offenders behind bars.

Ten Life Stages of the Insider Spy

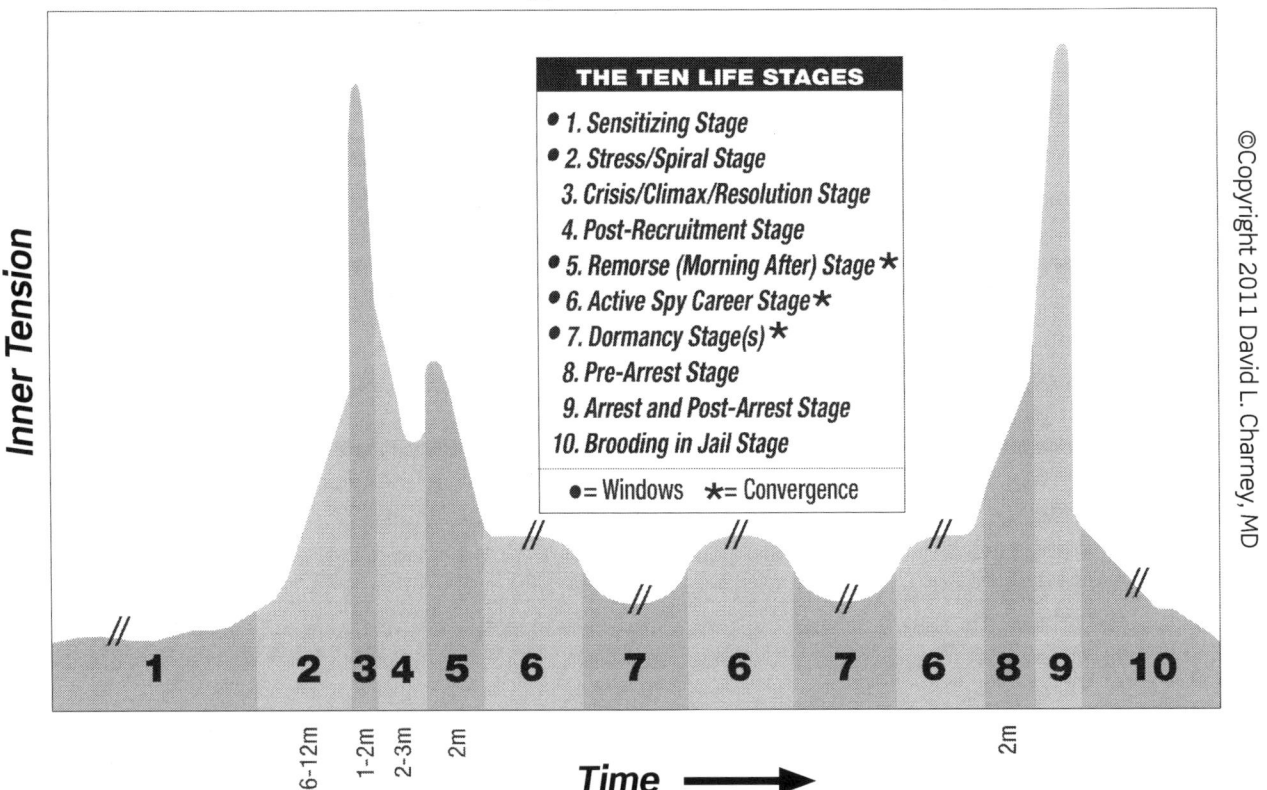

THE TEN LIFE STAGES

- ● 1. Sensitizing Stage
- ● 2. Stress/Spiral Stage
-    3. Crisis/Climax/Resolution Stage
-    4. Post-Recruitment Stage
- ● 5. Remorse (Morning After) Stage ★
- ● 6. Active Spy Career Stage ★
- ● 7. Dormancy Stage(s) ★
-    8. Pre-Arrest Stage
-    9. Arrest and Post-Arrest Stage
-   10. Brooding in Jail Stage

●= Windows ★= Convergence

Inner Tension (vertical axis)

1   2 3 4 5   6   7   6   7   6   8 9   10

6-12m 1-2m 2-3m 2m   2m

Time →

Advocates for modern amped-up detection methods claim that new and advanced technologies on the horizon will be game changers that will overcome the historical shortcomings of detection. I will explain why detection "on steroids" is not likely to move the needle that much.

SECTION C

THE NOIR WHITE PAPER SERIES ON INSIDER THREAT, COUNTERINTELLIGENCE, AND COUNTERESPIONAGE (CE)

NOIR WHITE PAPER PART ONE[2]

True Psychology of the Insider Spy addressed how to understand the fundamentals of the problem from the perspective of the psychology of the spy and the insider threat actor. This first paper introduced the concepts of the *Core Psychology of the Insider Spy* as well as the *Ten Life Stages of the Insider Spy*.

NOIR WHITE PAPER PART TWO[2]

NOIR: Proposing A New Policy for Improving National Security by Fixing the Problem of Insider Spies was intended to make practical use of my psychological findings. I proposed standing up the National Office for Intelligence Reconciliation (NOIR), essentially an off-ramp exit solution for *after* someone has crossed the line. NOIR would be a new mechanism to stop and then mitigate the damage our national security suffers due to uninterrupted espionage. I asserted that NOIR was a critical missing link in the IC security chain. Admittedly a controversial proposal, I knew NOIR could not be the entire solution on its own. NOIR did not adequately address a more important antecedent missing link in IC security chain failure: *How to prevent someone from crossing the line in the first place?*

NOIR WHITE PAPER PART THREE

This paper will examine in detail the most important missing link in IC security chains: *prevention*. Although prevention mechanisms do exist within the IC, they are relatively weak. I will recommend ways to make prevention stronger and work better.

THE VISION: A FULL SPECTRUM SOLUTION FOR MANAGING INSIDER THREAT

My first two white papers addressed how to better understand insider threat actors, when and how to intervene to reduce insider threat, and what resources are missing to get the job done.

The major proposal of my second white paper, NOIR, was to build an off-ramp exit solution for those who have *already* crossed the line. While NOIR capabilities do not yet exist, NOIR's core concepts can be carried over to engineer prevention solutions that will be more effective than current practices. This third white paper will propose off-ramp exit solutions for the situation *before* someone crosses the line.

All three white papers focus thinking on how to create a seamless suite of resources, *a full spectrum solution* for better managing insider threat, to include off-ramp exits for *before* and for *after* someone crosses the line.

SECTION D

RETHINKING INSIDER THREAT

EXTERNAL MANAGEMENT OF INSIDER THREAT (EMIT) VS. INTERNAL MANAGEMENT OF INSIDER THREAT (IMIT)

Introducing two complementary categories that advance a conceptual overview of insider threat management. For this discussion, insider threat actors, insider spies, and even "whistleblowers," will be considered as somewhat interchangeable because in the early stages, these outwardly different actors demonstrate *strikingly similar underlying psychologies.*

EXTERNAL MANAGEMENT OF INSIDER THREAT (EMIT)

EMIT targets insider threat suspects with efforts that are externally focused, surveillance-based, intrusive, invasive, and even coercive. Detection is the principal discipline that epitomizes EMIT. Detection has always been law enforcement's primary means of managing criminal threat.

EMIT involves active and continuous surveillance of the entire IC workforce, scrutinizing a broad range of external, outside indicators to figure out what is going on inside.

EMIT's challenge parallels the children's book *Where's Waldo?*[3] Within a vast crowd of good, law-abiding employees, there's a Bad Waldo: Find him! Detect him, catch him red-handed if possible, arrest him, prosecute him, and throw him in jail!

EMIT detection methods work to identify persons of concern by discovering behavioral indicators that hint of an inclination to cross the line or telltale indicators that someone has already crossed the line.

EMIT is based on what's done to subjects of interest. Suspects, known or unknown, are not offered the chance to cooperate and their permission is not requested. Rather, they are regarded as subjects to be hunted down. Clues are sought, behaviors observed, subjects are tracked until they are finally caught. Security measures and surveillance strategies can be adversarial, even antagonistic.

EMIT-inspired security measures include: Clearances; continuous evaluation (CE); repeat background investigations; polygraphs (polys); physical measures, such as fobs, passes, badges, Sensitive Compartmented Information Facilities (SCIFs), etc.; and mandatory procedural methods, such as passwords, biometrics, etc.

EMIT, from the warfighter's perspective, can be likened to air war: technical, prosecuted from a distance, remote, sterile, clean, abstract. However, though necessary and effective, air war is rarely able to win wars all by itself.

EMIT's consequences for suspects: When they get identified, what follows are adversarial confrontations; lawyers; prosecution; and ultimately, incarceration.

EMIT's attempts at prevention messages implicitly or overtly threaten and warn of dire punishments, delivered in authoritarian, sometimes scolding tones.

The IC almost exclusively relies on EMIT principles and has a limited appreciation for perhaps more important factors. The IC tends to lack sensitivity to the core psychology of insider threat actors, employees who are psychologically floundering, desperate, broken.

INTERNAL MANAGEMENT OF INSIDER THREAT (IMIT)

IMIT aims at changing the inner thoughts, attitudes, and mindsets of troubled IC employees to head off the worst developments, including crossing the line.

IMIT encourages IC employees to think about alternative ideas of how to manage their overwhelming life situations, which makes for healthier internal debate. Employees on the brink are persuaded to rethink their dark, hopeless assessments and open up their minds to new, more positive ways of handling their problems.

IMIT attempts to convince employees to reach for helping resources that are presented as free choices. Resources would be attractively packaged for their due consideration.

IMIT is not based on law enforcement principles.

IMIT wants no part of an aversive, coercive, Stasi[4]-like workplace environment.

IMIT operates in accord with a softer, subtler "inner game" as opposed to a harder, more adversarial "outer game." As opposed to threats and warnings, offers of help are put forward.

> **IMIT aims at changing the inner thoughts, attitudes, and mindsets of troubled IC employees to head off the worst developments, including crossing the line.**

IMIT, from the war fighter's perspective, can be likened to ground war: close up and personal, one-on-one, gritty, in-your-face. While benefiting from air war, ground war is the military arm almost always necessary to finalize conflicts to definitive conclusions.

IMIT requires no courts or lawyers, so there is more flexibility and maneuvering room.

IMIT saves time, energy, and money, including some of the expenses needed to prosecute, and incarcerate offenders. More important, IMIT interventions can head off disastrous treasonous acts along with the enormous costs that are associated with them.

IMIT sets up a very different, more cooperative transaction from the start, more of a problem-solving methodology.

IMIT's key distinction: IMIT does not focus on catching hidden offenders. Rather, troubled employees are encouraged to come forward on their own. *They voluntarily self-identify.*

HUMAN PSYCHOLOGY IS CENTRAL TO IMIT-BASED PREVENTION

■ SITUATIONS OF CONCERN

Before (and after) the decision is made to cross the line, the situation should be viewed from the perspective of a male IC employee (females, far less frequently cross the line), who feels overwhelmed, stuck, trapped, unhappy, with no way out of his worst-ever life predicament. Desperation sets up his risk for making poor decisions like crossing the line.

LEFT OF BOOM

"Left of Boom" is a popular expression within the IC, referring to heading off a disastrous event, like an IED exploding, before it happens. When the chain of events is charted along a timeline, by convention, the bad end result is shown on the right side, so the antecedent events that led to the disaster are "left of boom." Of course, far better to intervene "left of boom," so the bomb never gets to explode.

■ MODERN SALES PRACTICES ARE KEY FOR ACHIEVING "LEFT OF BOOM" INTERVENTIONS

At its root, the insider threat actor's problem is self-disappointment and loss of self-respect.

Taking this psychology of defeat and hopelessness into account is essential for accurately framing appeals.

IMIT-based offers derive their redemptive power from raising *hope*. Hope for rescue, for the chance to get a new start on life, for being able to snatch victory from the jaws of defeat. Potential insider threat actors, whether IC employees or cleared contractors, will be offered the option to take an off-ramp exit *before* making the decision to cross the line.

Soft sells as opposed to hard sells are the modern way. Employees can freely make their own choices to take the higher road. They will do so only if the rationales for choosing positive alternatives are safe, rational and well presented.

Solutions on offer cannot be viewed as demeaning. Honorable ways must be offered that restore self-respect. This can be achieved through respectful persuasion, not through messages presented in tones that are hostile, threatening, or coercive. Trying to engage hidden potential insider threat actors with accusative name-calling is a losing tactic. They are already in fight mode because that is their blueprint for trying to cover up their *intolerable sense of personal failure.* They are too well practiced with confrontation, so why fight a frontal engagement on their chosen turf?

Messaging must be aimed at meeting vulnerable employees where they are right now, "on the ledge." They must be spoken to in terms that will penetrate their mental turmoil in simple, understandable language. Their crushed spirits must be understood and acknowledged. Give them what they are missing. In a word: *Hope.*

EMIT vs. IMIT

FACTORS	EMIT	IMIT
Professional Identity	Police	Sales
Spirit of Professionals	Hunters	Farmers
Actions	Catch	Persuade
Manner of Engagement	Doing *to*	Doing *with*
Type of Cop	Bad Cop	Good Cop
Carrots and Sticks	Sticks Only	Carrots Too
Warfare Type	Air War	Ground War
Emotional Tone	Cold	Warm
Sensitivity to Psychology	Minimal	Maximal
Concerns About Subject's Family	None	Major
Change Subject's Thinking?	No	Yes
Subject's Decision	Involuntary	Voluntary
Identified How?	Detection	Self-identified
Highest Aim	Punish	Save
Ideally, How It Ends?	Incarceration	Back to Work
Where?	Bureau of Prisons	Home Agency
Ancillary Professionals	Lawyers, Judges	Counselors

■ NOT NEW! IMIT-BASED APPROACHES ALREADY PRACTICED IN SPECIALIZED IC UNITS

Methods using softer appeals with dangerous characters in tough life-or-death situations are not new to the IC. These alternative approaches are well known, accepted, and practiced by specialized government units such as FBI hostage negotiation teams and police department special weapons and tactics (SWAT) teams.

Basic Strategy with Hostage Takers:

- Build a human relationship, a bonding
- Start a conversation
- Stretch it out, keep it going for as long as possible

- Delay rushing into action, do anything to decrease tension
- Suggest many alternative options
- Avoid getting confrontational
- Offer comfort items: food, calls to friends or relatives
- Do not jump to using guns, risking killing hostages or bystanders; use guns only *in extremis.*

■ BEHAVIORAL CHANGE STAIRWAY MODEL[5]

The FBI developed this model. Police negotiators who follow this model work through the following stages strictly in order:

- **Active Listening:** Understand the psychology of the perpetrators; let them know they are being listened to

- **Empathy:** Understand their issues and how they feel

- **Rapport:** When negotiators begin to understand how the perpetrators feel, they build trust

- **Influence:** Only when trust has been gained can solutions to the perpetrators' problems be recommended

- **Behavioral Change:** Perpetrators act more responsibly and may surrender

Important: Working through these steps in proper sequence is key. Do not to try to effect behavioral change before rapport has been established.

This softer approach contrasts with older, more brute-force methods. In a parallel domain, for developing more effective interrogation techniques of captured terrorists, similar softer methods have evolved as the preferred approach.[6]

With insider threat actors, the hostage is not a person but rather the IC's precious classified national security secrets.

FULL SPECTRUM SOLUTION FOR MANAGING IC INSIDER THREAT REQUIRES EMIT AND IMIT

Detection approaches based on EMIT principles have been, thus far, the IC's nearly exclusive efforts to contain insider threat. Prevention, based mostly on IMIT principles, has been allocated far less thought and effort.

■ KEY POINTS:

- **EMIT-based detection is necessary but not sufficient**

- **IMIT-based prevention complements, *does not replace* EMIT-based detection**

- **Prevention addresses the situation *before* the decision gets made to cross the line, the most important missing link in the IC security chain**

- **Detection needs to be supplemented by adding off-ramp exit solutions**

- **Prevention provides the *front-end* off-ramp exit solution**

- **NOIR provides the *back-end* exit solution for *after* the decision gets made to cross the line**

■ GOALS OF THIS PAPER:

- To change the current situation, an almost exclusive reliance by the IC on EMIT

- To remedy the imbalance by adding IMIT tools to the arsenal

> ### Comment on *"Whistleblowers"*
> Proposals explored in this paper are designed to be effective not only with conventional state-sponsored insider spies but also with whistleblowers and other categories of insider threat actors.

SECTION E

DETECTION: STRENGTHS AND WEAKNESSES

DETECTION: CORE MISSION OF TRADITIONAL LAW ENFORCEMENT

Detection is at the core of the IC's DNA and has always been its most highly valued methodology. As mentioned, this is true despite what history shows: Detection has had only limited success in catching major spies. *Detection primarily focuses on finding employees who have already crossed the line but does not contribute much to keeping an employee from crossing the line in the first place.*

The IC has long experience and familiarity with detection approaches that come out of the world of law enforcement. Thus, detection operates right inside the IC's comfort zone. New proposals to improve detection usually amount to perpetuating the same timeworn practices, but promising to do them better, harder, faster, and amped up with modern high-tech tweaks. The newest proposals for improving detection do not capitalize on the expanded understanding of the psychology of insider spies and insider threat actors.

STRENGTHS OF DETECTION

Detection can provide early warning signals regarding employees of concern before they cross the line. In this respect, detection can overlap with prevention. Detection can identify malicious actors after they cross the line or at least can identify indicators of ongoing espionage.

Detection has always been the main approach for

managing insider threat precisely because it has demonstrated its many strengths since time immemorial. Detection strengths are so well known that listing them here in detail will add too much to an already lengthy paper. Highlighting an obvious point, detection's many strengths must be acknowledged.

WEAKNESSES OF DETECTION

■ FACTORS RELATED TO PRESENT DAY CONDITIONS

Exponentially Increased Risk Today

Classified documents are treated no differently these days than conventional documents: virtually all documents have shifted from paper to bits and bytes. Today, it is all zeros and ones. Massive amounts of classified material can be stolen using tiny thumb drives or other devices.[7]

More Hostile Foreign Intelligence Entity (FIE) Officers on the Prowl

Experts in the know state that more hostile FIE case officers are prowling around Washington today than during the height of the cold war.[8] If stealing secrets is now so easy to accomplish remotely via the internet, why do our adversaries bother to work so hard at conventional human agent recruitment? Our adversaries would not be doing this if they did not see the value. Flooding the field with operatives, they will probably succeed in recruiting and handling as recruitments in place (RIPs) more of our IC personnel. It is partly a numbers game. Human intelligence (HUMINT) is still alive and well and often outperforms technical intelligence.

Generational Changes

The latest generation entering the workforce may be more self-absorbed, less loyal to their employers, feel more entitled and empowered to make decisions based on their convictions, and may be less attuned to the larger consequences of their actions. Consequently, the number of breaches seems to have increased.[9]

■ INTRINSIC WEAKNESSES

Detection is Subject to the Iron Law of Diminishing Returns

The costs of improving detection methods tend to increase more rapidly than results get improved. How much more investment of time, energy, and money will it take to improve detection outcomes? Hundreds of millions of dollars to improve the catch rate of insider threat actors by only one or two percent?

■ WORKPLACE BARRIERS THAT THWART DETECTION

Coworkers find it hard to speak up.
No one wants to be a snitch! IC employees are reluctant to call out co-workers' behaviors of concern. Employees fear violating the culture of team spirit, trust, cohesion, sharing, and openness.

Moral reluctance.
Employees may feel it is presumptuous to assess and label others critically. That would be like casting stones. *Could I be next?*

Privacy concerns.
Employees do not want to cross lines of privacy and intrude into someone else's space.

Legal risks.
Suppose you are wrong? *Then what?*

Functional blindness.
This is the net result of these very human workplace barriers.

AN APPROACH THAT OVERCAME SIMILAR PROBLEMS: FAA STRATEGY TO DEAL WITH ALCOHOLIC PILOTS.

The FAA came up with a strategy to deal with the problem of alcoholic pilots. They knew other flight crew were reluctant to blow the whistle on alcoholic pilots because it might cost the pilots their jobs. They were afraid of being snitches.

The policy was revised to assure flight crews that if they did the right thing and turned in any alcoholic pilot, that pilot would not be fired. Instead, the pilot would be confronted and offered a chance to attend an aggressive alcohol treatment program. If they completed the program and its follow up treatment, they could fly again.

Sometimes a member of the flying public would hear about this program and be appalled: "You mean I could be flying with a recovering alcoholic pilot at the controls?!" The answer: "Would you rather be flying with an active alcoholic at the controls?"

Pervasive all-seeing surveillance regimes can backfire.
The atmosphere of ubiquitous surveillance degrades agency morale. Who wants to live in a workplace that resembles East Germany under the Stasi's omnipresent surveillance?

■ WORKFORCE HIRING PARADOXES WITHIN THE IC

IC's Claims About Its Ideal Hires

The IC ideally wants creative thinkers, unafraid to pursue new ideas, explore unusual sources, good at connecting dots, all in accordance with the vaunted post-9/11 lesson: "Beware the failure of imagination." Messy, complicated minds will be fine since they are useful for some aspects of analysis. The IC will have to grudgingly accept that private lives may be somewhat alternative.

What Really Happens? Paradoxical Results

With oppressive surveillance regimes, the qualities mentioned above would be discouraged. Different, imaginative, adventuresome types would be deselected or made unwelcome. They are too risky and dangerous! Oppressive work atmospheres are too constraining for these types – they will soon leave thinking: *Who needs it?* Oppressive surveillance regimes select for conventional, compliant, steady but unimaginative types, resulting in a workforce at the opposite pole from what was desired.

■ NET RESULT OF DETECTION WEAKNESSES:

Overly stringent detection surveillance regimes can cut two ways. Weighing security vs. competence, what is the right balance?

■ DETECTION IS NEARLY USELESS WITH "WHISTLEBLOWERS"

Detection may help if the potential whistleblower takes his time gathering his trove of classified materials so that his preparations may get noticed.

However, with impulsive actors moving rapidly, events can overtake detection methods. Sensitive materials can explode into public view with nothing left to detect!

Prevention, not detection, is the only way to head off whistleblowers.

■ PROBLEMS IN EXECUTION

"Solving" Problems: Appearances vs. Reality

Government tends to throw big money at tough problems for solutions that will not necessarily work. Senior management points with pride to closing new

"BIG IRON"

"Big Iron" was a term used by government contractors to describe massive hardware purchases, parts of the systems sold to the government that were claimed to solve incredibly complex problems. After tens or hundreds of millions of dollars were spent and nothing got solved, the machines were occasionally literally hidden away in the unhappy agency's subbasement to conceal the proof of the failure, thus hopefully sparing some of the embarrassment.

large contracts aimed at deterring insider threat. It shows "something is being done."

Contracts for developing and deploying complex new systems have long time horizons, subject to what one expert described as "The Conspiracy of Hope."[10] Interested parties pretend that everything will work just fine, another Washington example of "the triumph of hope over experience." Despite initial grandiose claims, when mega projects show minimal success, or when they prove to be outright failures, disappointing results somehow seem to disappear. Who pays attention and tracks these long-term projects? By the time contracts get close to completion, the original government plank holders have retired. Contractors still embedded in a project may be aware of the program's shortcomings but have career and economic stakes in calling it a success.

Many Washington stories tell of enormously expensive projects that came to naught. It used to be called "Big Iron," hidden out of sight in the basement.

■ FALSE NEGATIVES, FALSE POSITIVES, AND OTHER CONFUSING OR BAD RESULTS

False Negatives
Failure to identify insider threat actors and their activities. They just do not show up on the radar.

False Positives
Misidentification of innocent employees as being malicious insiders or insider spies.

■ CONSEQUENCES

False positives adversely impact agency coworkers when they personally know the "suspect" and the allegations do not add up. They worry: *That makes no sense. Who will be caught the next time the music stops? Me?*

Brian Kelley was a true American patriot, possessing the highest level of professional integrity. Nevertheless, the FBI decided that he fit the parameters of a mole suspected to be operating within the CIA. Ironically, this was partly based on Kelley having solved the case of State Department Foreign Service Officer Felix Bloch. Kelley used his unique brand of detection analysis and solved one of the very few insider spy cases based on shrewd detection. Unfortunately, that success was twisted as evidence to be used against him.

There were other breathtaking errors, including finding a map at Kelley's house that was interpreted as locating drop sites in the park nearby. Except it was really Kelley's jogging map!

Kelley and his family were subjected to high pressure for over three years. Kelley never cracked, which was seen as further proof that he must be a *master spy.*

After a long ordeal, lo and behold, as it usually happens, a former KGB officer came over with information indicating that the spy was actually one of the FBI's own, Special Agent Robert Hanssen.

Washington is a surprisingly small town. Brian Kelly was my friend. How can one explain the amazing coincidence that Brian Kelley got suspected to be the spy that Robert Hanssen actually was? And that I wound up being the psychiatrist who worked with Robert Hanssen for a full year in jail after he was caught?

I listened to hours of hurt and pain Brian Kelley expressed to me from time to time. However, Brian took the high road and never sued the government. He just wanted to get back to his job in CIA counterintelligence and teach and mentor to the rising generation of new intelligence officers. He was appreciated and loved by his many students and protégés. Sadly, I believe the stress of it all led to his untimely death. False positives are *not* trivial!

These situations can degrade morale. Many employees are made chronically insecure, edgy, and nervous.

Personnel consequences can be expensive. Careers can be ruined when someone erroneously gets relegated to the penalty box. Losing highly selected, trained, and experienced personnel with not easily replicated specialized skill sets imposes high costs: to recruit, clear, hire, train, and replace key personnel. Also, it costs time to get back up to speed.

Frustrating Situations:
Example of the Felix Bloch Case

Bloch was known to be a spy. However, once he was alerted that he was under suspicion, he made sure not to get caught red-handed. Bloch fell into the non-prosecutable category. The IC's hands were tied. *Now what?*

- No solid confirmation of Bloch's spying
- Bloch could not be prosecuted
- Nothing was left to do
- The IC's last resort? Merely harassing Bloch
- The IC was left frustrated because the most valuable asset to be gained from a captured spy, a full damage assessment, was out of reach

LOOKING AHEAD: EXCESSIVELY OPTIMISTIC CLAIMS FOR NEW HIGH-TECH ADVANCES

ARTIFICIAL INTELLIGENCE (AI), BIG DATA, ALGORITHMS, AND MACHINE LEARNING (ML)

When examined more closely, advanced methods such as high-tech surveillance, AI, big data, algorithms, and ML are unlikely to deliver "slam dunks" regarding identifying insider threat actors or guiding what to do with alleged suspects.

AI, big data, algorithms, and ML operate autonomously and make decisions based on obscure algorithms employing unknown criteria, not necessarily based on anything resembling sound human judgment. This supposed advantage could conceal significant flaws.[11] Algorithms can contain hidden biases that distort results.

ALGORITHM BIAS: A NEWLY NAMED CONCEPT[12]

This refers to hidden biases built into algorithms, also called Unconscious Bias. Once baked in, there is no way to know what criteria were used to generate results. System designers tend to be reluctant to find and fix these biases. This revisits the computer world's perennial problem of garbage in/garbage out (GIGO). Lack of clarity and transparency regarding the obscure parameters that figure into machine-generated decisions means that findings can be just plain wrong, thus, easily challenged. Unfortunately, this can lead to bad judgment calls and follow-on consequences since the personal stakes are high for employees who come under suspicion. How much confidence can there be when the ML "black box" kicks out its conclusions? Right or wrong, findings can and will be challenged.

PARADIGM OF HOME SECURITY SYSTEMS

The art and science of setting threshold sensitivities of home security system window sensors demonstrates that *setting the sensor threshold is key*. If the threshold is set too high (insensitive), then even someone breaking in will not be enough to set off the alarm. If the threshold is set too low (overly sensitive), then any passing wind can set off the alarm. When police come the second time, they are annoyed. The *third* time, they may give you a fine.

THRESHOLDS IN THE CONTEXT OF THE IC

If thresholds are set too high, there will be false negatives and real cases will be missed. If thresholds are set too low, there will be false positives, with unfair and ruinous career consequences for innocent employees.

Also, an enormous number of employees are likely to come under suspicion so that impossibly large caseloads will now require clearance. All suspects will have to be processed, interfering with mission as suspects get sidelined during lengthy clearance reinvestigations.

There is no way to achieve a perfect threshold setting.

The only recourse: Determine an optimal threshold, based on tradeoffs and compromises, and then periodically readjust. Which is a nice way of saying it is not so much pure science as having to make *human judgment calls.*

DEFINING SUSPECTS BASED ON AN ALGORITHM

■ *AN INSIDER THREAT SCORE?*

Specific cutoff numbers, or segments of the population that raise concern? The software will determine the edges between different segments and will amplify edge contrast, sharpening small differences. Result: the illusion of precision.

■ *ARBITRARY THRESHOLDS TEND TO GET TURNED INTO CONCRETE CATEGORIES*

What began as reasonable theoretical models for defining "persons of interest" will get operationalized by bureaucracies into categorical guidelines that may not make real world sense. Imagine this conversation:

"Jim, I know you are a good guy, but the machine just told me you are a risk. I feel terrible about it, but for now, you have to leave our office."

CONGRATULATIONS! YOU IDENTIFIED A SUSPECT. NOW WHAT?

■ *HIGH-TECH INDICATORS: HELPFUL OR PROBLEMATIC?*

When the algorithm kicks out a precise numeric score, "a scientific assessment" that sharply meets the (arbitrary) threshold you or the machine set for defining insider threat concern, the issue promptly converts to a strictly human judgment call: *What do you do next, how do you handle it?*

■ *PARALLELS THE PROBLEM OF WHAT TO DO WITH WEATHER FORECASTS*

"Today, there is a 30 percent chance of rain."

Sounds very scientific. This seemingly precise percentage does not provide you with a clear answer to your practical question. It still falls to your judgment, your estimate of risk, and risk tolerance, as to what to make of the percent quoted.

Do you or do you not lug around your umbrella today?

■ *BRING IN THE BIG GUNS: THE FBI WILL SOLVE IT!*

Not so fast. Now another bureaucracy is in the decision mix with its lengthy timelines and obscure protocols. FBI Special Agents can have their own reasons to drag out investigations.

First, Special Agents are busy with other, perhaps genuinely more pressing matters.

Second, Special Agents become parties with their own interests. FBI personnel have their own stakes in the game, namely, protecting their own careers. Why risk reputation on behalf of an uncertain IC employee, when clearing that person may later prove to have been the wrong call? It is easier and safer to avoid clearing anyone who is remotely suspicious. The clearance process is not transparent so there is little risk attached to delaying or denying clearance. Who can challenge delays or outright clearance denials when the mysterious process hinges on unknown classified details?

When clearance decisions do not come quickly, other costs get imposed. As they say in legal circles: "Justice delayed is justice denied."

■ HASSLES MANAGING SUSPECTS

- How will each risk segment be managed compared to the others? Why?
- What about someone on the boundary line between segments?
- How will individual suspects be handled?
- Direct interrogations? Secret investigations?

What if there are too many suspects to investigate?

There will probably be many false positives, which, as mentioned, can overwhelm the entire security clearance system. Consequences include sidelining too many key personnel, which can degrade fulfilling critical missions.

"FAILING THE POLY": AN EXAMPLE OF HOW REAL-LIFE SITUATIONS GOT MESSY

How "failed polys" were handled:

Any result that was not a definite pass led to follow-up FBI investigations that could last for years.

Typical explanations that were given by security for sidelining employees: "We take many factors into consideration. The poly is just one tool."

No, it wasn't.

It was a career killer.

My experience with about a dozen CIA employees who "failed the poly":

Not one stood out as a traitor.

Some were genuine heroes who sacrificed much for our country.

Nearly all had either hard life experiences that sensitized them, or had obsessional worry about minor or inconsequential details. In short, most were worrywarts who overthought things.

How were these problematic employees handled?

They were no longer "worldwide eligible," therefore, they were no longer promotable. But they were retained in their current jobs, usually with continued access to classified materials. They were neither fish nor fowl. How confusing!

Sidelined employees typically chose to put up with their limbo status and stayed in their jobs because they had so much invested in their careers, and of course, they needed to protect their retirements. They were forced to "retire in place" well before their actual retirement date.

This created a class of hurt, disgruntled, angry, and bitter employees, the very class of employees you do not want to be working in your agency. This paradoxical result was the opposite of what was intended. Employees were transformed into the same reservoir of unhappy people from which insider spies get recruited!

Possible remedy: Change the threshold criteria?

Then it becomes even more transparently arbitrary and subject to challenge.

Confront, counsel, or hold back?
Damned if you do, damned if you don't.

You cannot ignore suspicious behaviors because that would implicitly give the green light for such an employee to keep doing his sketchy activities. If you do confront him, it can be the very trigger that causes the worst outcomes you most fear. What if a confrontation annoys or even outrages a suspect and becomes the very predicate for tipping him over to finally commit a treasonous act?

These are the "hot potato" scenarios, where you are damned if you do and damned if you don't – the very problems that Judge William Webster identified as what kept him awake at night.[13]

DESPITE THE HYPE, HIGH TECH OFFERS LITTLE RELIEF FOR DECISION MAKERS

Results from high-tech surveillance findings do not relieve decision makers of the problem of what to do with the results, how to handle specific cases. Human beings, not machines or algorithms, still must make the hard decisions.

Clinton's Arkansas story

After winning his first presidential election, to explain how he now felt, Bill Clinton told his Arkansas story of the dog that chased a pickup truck all through town. When the dog finally caught up with the pickup truck, it had no idea what to do next!

It is the same thing when you identify an insider threat suspect. *Now what?*

DEFEATING THE NEWEST DETECTION TECHNOLOGY? "ZERO DAYS" ARE EVERY DAY

Determined insiders can and will defeat any security technology devised. It takes years and enormous cost to conceive and build advanced technology systems that are secure, with built-in detection components, which gives plenty of time for motivated hackers and insider threat actors to figure out how to defeat them. Also, after any such new system finally gets deployed, its details inevitably leak out. Determined insider threat actors will soon find a way to exploit them. Naïve insiders who try to breach these systems may get snared, but not the more sophisticated and dangerous insiders.

This situation resembles the age-old back and forth cycles experienced with any new "super weapon." Soon after its deployment, the next advancement in defensive countermeasures neutralizes the latest super weapon. Then it recycles again and again.

Exceptions showing the best protections can be overcome

Ronald Pelton and Anna Montes were insider spies, but neither of them needed physical documents. They both had photographic memories and walked out with everything memorized!

What everybody in the information technology (IT) world knows

Someone in their mother's basement anywhere in the world can penetrate the most secure computer system. Sophisticated IT experts no longer promise perfect protection from intrusions. They are resigned to the fact that any system can eventually be penetrated. They now talk about managing risk, making decisions of what to protect, with what levels of defense considering the costs, and how to build resilient capabilities to mitigate penetrations when they inevitably occur.

Cycle Times and OODA Loops

With massively complex high-tech security systems, as each new intrusion threat materializes, there is limited agility to devise protective fixes and workarounds. By the time a new fix gets fielded, hackers have moved on to exploit the next vulnerability they have already discovered. OODA Loop cycle times ("Observe, Orient, Decide, Act") that are too slow will prevent getting ahead of the curve. Never a good night's sleep for security experts!

> **OODA LOOPS**
>
> United States Air Force officer John Boyd developed the concept of OODA Loops.
>
> I was introduced to Boyd's ideas by a surprising source: the spy Robert Hanssen! This illustrates the complexity of human beings. On the one hand, Hanssen was a Russian spy. On the other hand, he regarded himself as a loyal American and tried to improve and strengthen the capabilities of the FBI, for which he worked.
>
> Hanssen told me that he found no interest within the FBI to learn anything from Boyd. This rejection of Hanssen's potentially valuable contribution to the FBI was yet one more hurt that added to his alienation.

Continuous Evaluation (CE)

The latest miracle cure, CE, proposes to rely on many of the high-tech detection activities described above. In theory, bad actors cannot avoid leaving a trail of breadcrumbs that will disclose their malicious behavior. These indicators will be picked up by any number of sensors, to include the latest internet of things (IoT) technologies.

We can comfortably assume that smart and well-motivated malefactors will quickly wise up about these technologies and adapt their behavior to operate under the radar. Strategies and tactics of how to defeat many of the newest technologies are staples of modern military thriller novels. If novelists can invent clever ways to evade or counteract any new, brilliant high-tech system, real insider threat actors will be even more motivated.

Example: Proving the Point

After briefing a CIA group, I met someone from the Directorate of Science and Technology (DS&T), who laughed when he heard about claims that were made regarding the latest, supposedly impregnable system. He told me: "Give me a few hours and I'll defeat any new thing you put in front of me. I don't want to do it. But if I *did* want to do it, believe me, *I could do it!*"

> "Give me a few hours and I'll defeat any new thing you put in front of me. I don't want to do it. But if I *did* want to do it, believe me, *I could do it!*"

Adding to the CE problems already discussed, extreme surveillance regimes can backfire by driving away the most desirable members of the future IC workforce. As prospective IC employees learn more about CE, they may get turned off and pass on ever applying for an IC job. Or if they do come on board, eventually out of sheer annoyance, they may decide to quit. Detection in the form of CE, while it may add more strength to deterring insider threat, may also turn out to be a cure that is worse than the disease. Once again, CE, like other detection methodologies, is a double-edged sword.

Message to Designers of Detection Systems, Including CE:

- You are smart, but you are not that smart
- Your adversaries are smarter
- They have all day to figure out how to beat your system
- You can never think of every which way to block their creative brilliance
- Read the news and learn about the latest penetration of any system you can name
- They are smarter. That is why you hired them in the first place

BIG PICTURE CONSIDERATIONS: IMIT ADVANTAGES OVER EMIT

EASIER DECISIONS

EMIT and detection methods make for difficult decision-making about insider threat suspects because they are grounded on the many uncertain, ambiguous premises mentioned above. IMIT mostly avoids these problems. IMIT makes life easier. There is no need to make hard calls based on imprecise indicators since IMIT is based on *voluntary self-identification*. Whether before or after crossing the line, the person of interest *shows up on his own*. Thus, no ambiguity.

Subjects who *voluntarily self-identify* simplify the problem because no elaborate detection efforts are required. Dangerous developments get short circuited earlier. That said, self-identified subjects must still be handled carefully and sensitively. By definition, they are still contending with major life stresses, still in a state of mental turmoil and overwhelmed by turbulent emotions.

CHEAPER

Standing up IMIT resources is less expensive than EMIT (but still not cheap).

IMIT cost accounting:

First, savings from scaling back some of the high costs of elaborate new detection systems can counterbalance some of the costs of IMIT. Of course, EMIT efforts must be kept robust since they will always be critically important. That said, overreliance on EMIT is the issue. The relative neglect of IMIT efforts needs to be addressed. Allocation of IC resources and effort has to be rebalanced.

Second, and most important, IMIT costs will be offset by stopping or mitigating major harms to our national security *that will never come to be.*

FASTER

Detection can take a very long time before subjects get identified. Since nearly all major spy cases do not get solved until someone from the other side crosses over to our side, the timing of that happy event is utterly unpredictable. While active counterintelligence and foreign intelligence recruitment in place (RIP) operations are always ongoing, it boils down to hoping something good will happen and happen quickly. *Hope is not a strategy.*

EASIER TO MANAGE

It is easier to manage voluntary, self-identified, relatively cooperative employees who turn themselves in, as compared to employees who were caught because of detection and who are now disappointed, fearful, and angry. Voluntary, self-identified employees are less likely to be vengeful and defiant. They are less liable to focus on the idea that the IC is their enemy. Since they chose to step forward on their own, they are more likely to recognize and admit to their deficiencies and poor choices, more likely to be ready to refocus on seeking paths to recovery.

IMIT approaches are supportive of an impaired employee's need to restore his sense of dignity, self-respect, pride, and manliness. He will take comfort from knowing that the IC recognizes and respects his real needs.

A troubled employee's core intention was probably never to harm the national security of the United States. His fundamental problem was mainly an internal personal crisis that played itself out in the workplace setting.

RESCUE VS. CATCH

In many cases, IMIT approaches will be able to save good employees who nearly went astray and return them to useful work.

SADLY, NOT EVERY TROUBLED EMPLOYEE WILL BE RESCUABLE

In which case, the proposed NOIR mechanism would be helpful to have already in place, ready as a backup option and alternative off-ramp exit solution, if needed.

SUMMING UP:

- *IMIT confers advantages over EMIT for managing insider threat both before and after crossing the line.*

- *EMIT still remains the bedrock foundation for robust multilayered defenses against insider threat.*

SECTION F

PREVENTION: STRENGTHS AND WEAKNESSES

STRENGTHS OF CURRENT PRACTICES

Prevention elements that do work well, often combined with elements of detection:

- Thorough initial vetting before hire
- Security training during onboarding
- Periodic reinvestigations
- Repeat polys
- Continuous technology-based surveillance
- Physical security measures such as SCIFs, biometric identification, etc.
- Routine security procedures, such as passwords, ID passes, fobs, two-person protocols, and numerous other EMIT security practices

WEAKNESSES OF CURRENT PRACTICES

■ CULTURAL: PREVENTION IS THE STEPCHILD OF COUNTERINTELLIGENCE

Detection is the preferred mindset of the IC. Just detection. Prevention runs against the grain, the DNA, of the IC. *Prevention gets no love. Detection gets all the love.* For the IC, prevention is not as stimulating nor as satisfying as detection. IC personnel see themselves more as Hunters than as Farmers.

The IC's strategy has been to do what the IC knows how to do best, not necessarily what is also needed to be done. Few in the IC know how to do anything besides detection. They believe they just need to be good Hunters.

HUNTERS AND FARMERS

Hunters and Farmers is one way to frame an understanding of how different brains work as understood within the psychiatric field of attention deficit disorder (ADD).

Hunters became a shorthand way of describing many with ADD whose style of coping depends on quick assessments, ability to shift focus rapidly, connect dots that others may miss, etc. In other words, even though ADD tends to be viewed in modern life as somewhat of a disability, these very same ADD traits during a hunt can be adaptive, useful and bring success.

By contrast, Farmers are slower, more detailed in their planning, must patiently deal with very long-term time horizons. Agriculture and the rise of civilization required these other types of minds.

I repurposed this dichotomy, Hunters vs. Farmers, used to better understand ADD, to help in rethinking insider threat management.

Familiarity with these novel conceptual simplifications, Hunters and Farmers, led me to reuse and adapt them for thinking about the different approaches that can be taken in the management of insider threat.

The IC does not know how to do fully effective prevention, which is more like Farming. The IC needs to cultivate Farming expertise too. Farming is what made mankind and civilization flourish, coaxing food out the ground using correct methods and timing, as dictated by nature. Hunting, always important, came to be recognized as having its limitations. Farming strengths began to surpass Hunter strengths.

"Farming" is the metaphor used here for gently coaxing employees "off the ledge" when they have moved beyond their capacities to cope with their disordered lives, so they will not go on to cross the line.

■ MEASURING SUCCESS: PREVENTION'S BIGGEST PROBLEM

Defining prevention success is hard. How do you know for sure if prevention efforts have worked when the measure of success is counting something bad that *did not* happen?

What do you count to prove success?

Einstein reputedly said: *"Not everything that counts can be counted and not everything that can be counted counts."*

Measuring success is hard when there is limited knowledge of a problem's baseline prevalence. All we know is how many insider spies have been caught. However, who believes that number represents a full accounting of the true number of insider spies? Optimistically, maybe there are only a few more out there than the number caught. Or, pessimistically, there may be multitudes still hidden away in the woodwork. The actual number remains a mystery.

■ PREVENTION RESOURCES TODAY NEED STRENGTHENING

The primary resources within each IC agency for prevention today are the employee assistance programs (EAPs) under their various IC agency names. Unfortunately, these EAP resources are not set up to manage the most serious cases, the very cases for which help is most needed to head off insider threat events. Let's consider the classes of possible EAP users:

The Three Classes of Troubled Employees

Class A
- Minor problem levels
- More stable individuals in minor crises who voluntarily seek counseling
- Existing EAPs can work with them

Class B
- Medium problem levels
- Behavioral indicators of distress visibly leak out, so managers pressure them to get counseling
- Troubled individuals are required to go to EAP
- Sometimes EAP can help with these cases

Class C
- Most serious problem levels
- Employees in serious trouble who can somehow conceal their distress. No one can see them sweat

- They are also the ones who can do the worst damage

- These are the employees who don't dare show up at EAPs! They are familiar with the EAPs' corridor reputation: If they go to an EAP, the next thing that will happen is a call from their friendly security officer

- Next on the agenda will be these bad consequences:

    - Loss of their clearance

    - Loss of their hopes for promotion

    - Loss of a portion of their income

    - Loss of their job

Stories Heard from the Corridor

Sometimes State Department diplomatic security agents do not dare reach for help. They correctly fear that their hopes for promotion will be taken off the table. If they are no longer allowed to carry their weapons, they know they will immediately lose 25% of their pay.

Some National Security Agency (NSA) managers have been known to explicitly warn subordinates *not* to seek help. They helpfully explain that it will become a nightmare for the troubled officers (true), but even worse, for themselves too.

Net Result:

Employees of greatest concern, with the most serious problems, are the very ones who will not dare make the call for help and will never show up at their home agency's EAP. How do you spell "disincentive?"

EAPs Today Are Like Urgent Care Centers

Urgent care centers, also known as "docs-in-the-box," have sprung up everywhere because in the medical world they satisfy a market need. They are cheaper, quicker, nearby, and handy, with locations everywhere.

Urgent care centers are very useful but are limited in what they can treat depending on severity of condition. They are geared up to deal with minor illnesses and some medium-level medical concerns. For medically dire situations, like severe trauma or life-threatening illnesses, there is no substitute for a full-fledged emergency room.

EAPs, like urgent care centers, are incapable of serving the most serious cases within the IC: Employees who are struggling with personal crises equivalent to major medical emergencies. That is because EAPs *are not perceived to be safe resources.* EAPs are there in the org chart ("We've taken care of that"), but they do not provide help for the very cases for which they are most needed. EAPs are good for Class A and even Class B, but not Class C employees.

SUMMARIZING:

In the IC, we have urgent care centers, but no full-fledged emergency rooms necessary for the ones who need it most: Class C employees.

SECTION G

BUILDING A NEW COMPREHENSIVE PREVENTION PROGRAM

GENERAL CONSIDERATIONS

■ IMIT CONCEPTS WILL BE ITS GUIDING PRINCIPLES

Key Concern: Safety is Number One

Resources that are not perceived as safe are the same as no resources.

Anyone in big trouble today understandably fears seeking help because they worry it will only make things worse. They are concerned that communication between their home agency's EAP and their security and counterintelligence components is too direct, free, and easy.

Safe, government-sanctioned, confidential help would make all the difference. Only if such resources were seen as trustworthy and practical would employees consider it worthwhile to take the risk and give them a try.

"Lean on Me"

"Lean on Me" is a song that communicates a warm and caring invitation for accepting help, especially aimed at men whose pride tends to get in the way.[14]

Initial Contact: Making It Safe

For anyone overwhelmed by serious problems, it will be scary merely to explore the possibility of starting to seek help and counseling. Before getting started in earnest, there would have to be a delicate dance of exploratory contacts designed to be very secure.

Off-Ramp Exits Needed *Before* Someone Crosses the Line

Well-crafted off-ramp exit solutions will work if based on sound psychological principles. This requires in-depth understanding of the psychology of the target audience: Men undergoing the worst personal crises of their lives who feel like they are drowning.

Rapid

Interventions cannot be slow moving. Fast pacing is key. Interventions must immediately relieve the pressure so employees can quickly work their way out of their *Psychological Perfect Storms*. Think of helping a drowning person climb out of a raging river to the safety of the riverbank. Only once he feels safe will he be able to catch his breath and start to think clearly again.

Remove All Barriers

Barriers to entry need to be lowered to zero.
The price must be right: Free.

By removing any excuses to avoid reaching out for help, including financial, good things can start to happen. If there were no costs, there would be no excuses.

Comprehensive and Practical

EAP personnel will have to fix whatever needs fixing — and right away. Whatever it takes. Help must be provided across all areas of need, including financial.

EAPs must be delegated authority to effect or negotiate changes, including in the work setting:

- Leaves of absence
- Reduced work hours
- Change of work unit
- Change of supervisor
- Medical referral
- Marital counseling
- Help with children
- Anything else necessary

USEFUL STARTING FACT: ABOUT 90% OF INSIDER THREAT ACTORS ARE MALE

Males constitute about 90% of caught spies.

As a medical doctor, I am proud to announce that I discovered the genetic marker for insider spies: The Y chromosome.

This fact alone provides a valuable edge: the ability to sharply target messaging to the correct audience: to men, not so much to women. Therefore, understanding male psychology becomes key. Please read my *White Paper: Part One: True Psychology of the Insider Spy*, for a complete treatment of this subject.

INTERVENTION WINDOWS: WHEN OPEN AND WHEN CLOSED?

■ INTRODUCTION

For timing interventions, it is important to head off crossing the line in the "foothills" of the process, before it shoots up into the "mountains." By then, the process will have advanced too far, and potential insider threat actors will have become too alienated and impervious to corrective messaging.

Training and education efforts that set the stage for effective prevention are best timed to occur before Stage 2, the Stress/Spiral Stage, while the target audience is still functional, rational and open to influence, well before the decision to spy gets made.

TEN LIFE STAGES OF THE INSIDER SPY

Stage One: The Sensitizing Stage (Everyone experiences adversity)

Stage Two: The Stress/Spiral Stage (Psychological Perfect Storm)

Stage Three: The Crisis/Climax/Resolution Stage (Epiphany of a Solution)

Stage Four: The Post-Recruitment Stage (Euphoria, Learning Tradecraft)

Stage Five: The Remorse / Morning-After Stage ("What was I thinking? What have I done?")

Stage Six: The Active Spy Career Stage (Rationalizations, Constant Stress, Drudgery)

Stage Seven: The Dormancy Stage(s) (Fantasy of Escaping)

Stage Eight: The Pre-Arrest Stage ("Let's get it over with!")

Stage Nine: The Arrest and Post-Arrest Stage (Insolence, Belligerence but really Shame)

Stage Ten: The Brooding in Jail Stage (Sadder, Wiser, Philosophical)

■ FIRST OPEN WINDOW:
STAGE 2 (STRESS/SPIRAL STAGE):
BEFORE SOMEONE CROSSES THE LINE

The prelude to crossing the line consists of gradual shifts in the thinking of severely stressed and vulnerable individuals experiencing life pressures that pile up beyond their capacities to manage. This is an internal process, deliberately kept invisible to observers because of male pride – no one wants to let anyone else see them sweat.

If their thinking progresses to consider more extreme and desperate survival efforts, it starts to resemble falling into quicksand: the more they struggle, the more they sink even deeper, and the more they panic. That is when dangerous, irrational ideas of how to rescue themselves start to fill their minds – epiphanies of how to brilliantly solve every aspect of the terrible fixes they are in – by undertaking the drastic act of crossing the line.

■ INTERVENING DURING EARLY
AND MID-STAGE 2

Since it is still early in the progression, this is the ideal time to communicate corrective messages that offer well-packaged help. This is the last window of opportunity to do so before an employee finally decides to cross the line.

Once an employee progresses past some indefinable transition point, it is too late. The window closes. Their *personal psychological bubble* becomes impervious to rational guidance and restraint.

■ CLOSED WINDOWS:
STAGES 3 AND 4: THE BLACKOUT PERIODS

Windows are closed from just before to during and immediately after the decision to cross the line. During Stage 3 (Crisis, Climax, and Resolution Stage) and Stage 4 (Post-Recruitment Stage), the employee who is teetering on the edge of readiness to cross the line, or has just actually done so, is too flushed with excitement and misguided purpose. Temporarily, nothing can penetrate his agitated state, he is in a feverish, altered reality and can no longer exercise clear judgment. Thus, there is no power to intervene.

■ OPEN WINDOWS:
STAGE 5 (REMORSE, MORNING AFTER STAGE);
STAGE 6 (ACTIVE SPY CAREER STAGE); AND
STAGE 7 (DORMANCY STAGE):
THE STAGES AFTER SOMEONE CROSSES THE LINE

The heat of the moment will subside some months after having crossed the line, at which point the insider spy may realize he has made a terrible mistake. He recognizes he is stuck, trapped, and helpless, with no way out. These are the stages where an off-ramp exit option, the proposed NOIR mechanism, can offer a pathway out, which will stop the hemorrhage of our national security secrets.

See my *NOIR White Paper: Part Two* for a detailed explanation of these off-ramp options.

TWO-TIER STRUCTURE ADVOCATED FOR EAPS

■ FIRST TIER: EXISTING EAPS INTERNAL
TO EACH IC AGENCY

Main improvements needed to shore up existing internal EAPs include:

- More robust outreach to employees made with communications that align with the recommendations that are described below

- Firewalling of agency EAPs from management, security, and CI components

Advantages

Internal EAP personnel know their own agency culture intimately and have relationships with other home agency personnel, including management at all echelons. They are logistically handy since they are located on the premises.

Disadvantages

Internal EAPs tend not be trusted if there is a history of too much direct, free and easy communication with their home agency's security and CI components. Employees may be concerned about showing up on the premises of their internal EAP and run into people they know: "Jim, what are you doing here?"

After initial crisis management, employees may have to be turned over to another counselor for more long-term help. They may have to engage with a new person they may not like. They may need to tell their whole story all over again.

■ SECOND TIER: A SECOND-LEVEL EAP — EXTERNAL TO THE HOME AGENCY

This option could be thought of as an EAP "at a higher level." Standing up this new resource is essential because negative corridor reputations are hard to overcome. If an employee has a significant problem with their home agency, they will not expect to be treated fairly by its EAP. *They just will not go there.* If employees do not trust their home agency's EAP, they absolutely need an external EAP!

Advantages

An External EAP may be perceived as more trustworthy and safer regarding confidentiality simply because it is not attached to their home agency.

Disadvantages

External EAPs are less convenient since they are located further away.

External EAPs may not understand the inner workings of the home agency as well as internal EAPs.

RESOURCES MUST BE REAL

To truly fulfill promises to help, the IC cannot make promises that are not kept.

Resources offered need to go beyond psychological counseling.

They must also provide the following kinds of counseling:

- Financial, including easy loans
- Legal
- Tax and accounting
- Career counseling
- Guidance addressing any major life stresses

■ AN EXTERNAL EAP HAS THE ADVANTAGES OF A THIRD PARTY

As a third party, an external EAP provides a safer outlet since it is a step removed from the home agency. That distance makes it easier to vent and burn off intense negative feelings that troubled employees may harbor towards their distrusted home agency. A neutral third party can absorb hostile emotions based on bad experiences with antagonists within the employee's home agency, thus acting as a pressure release valve. As a government-sanctioned IC resource, the external EAP would be seen as safe since cleared counselors would staff it.

The external EAP's role would emulate private sector outplacement firms. Their job is to solve employee problems, and if necessary, ease them out — *but gently, gracefully and respectfully.* The aim is for "soft landings," which benefits the employee and the company.

■ RESOURCES

What is Needed and Why

Resources should be aimed at relieving the desperate employee's feeling of drowning *as soon as possible*, doing whatever it takes, whether problems are financial, relationship or work-based. A quick and immediate fix is critical. Afterward, there must be follow up with more careful long-term intervention for further repair and healing.

Cost considerations must be made subordinate to the larger goal of prevention. All it takes is one Hanssen or Snowden to underscore that the cost tradeoffs are clear: How many billions of dollars did it take

How many billions of dollars did it take to repair the damages of just these two insiders?

to repair the damages of just these two insiders?

More on costs: It is important for the IC to keep its eye on the ball. To illustrate this critical point, imagine a genie who says: *"I'm willing to turn the clock back to just before Snowden (or Hanssen, etc.) gave away all your precious secrets. You won't have lost any of them! How much would you be willing to pay?"*

Setting Up Resources Will Not Be Simple

Staffing Personnel Will Be Challenging

Recruiting, vetting and selecting counseling staff who meet demanding criteria:

- Experienced in the counseling field
- Familiar with the IC
- Understand the mission
- Engaging, warm, and personable

- Non-judgmental
- Practical
- Possesses skills to extend crisis counseling into longer-term follow-up

Specialized Training Will Be Needed

To handle "hot potato" cases, relieving the pressure rapidly.

Authorities

Staff will need to be given authority to make decisions and initiate actions that get the job done at whatever the cost—because the costs of failure to contain problem employees are likely to be vastly more than the costs of not heading off the threats. "Pennywise and pound-foolish" in these matters makes no sense.

Primary Aim: Rescue a basically good employee and get him back to work.

Separation from service must remain an option

Separation, in some cases, will be the better choice. Some employees will not be rescuable. Exercising this option would have to be carefully orchestrated to achieve the desired "soft landing." The proposed NOIR mechanism would be best for managing this outcome. For this reason, there is a rationale to simultaneously stand up both the proposed prevention resources, as well as NOIR, because the combination of both would create a seamless suite of off-ramp exit solutions, for the situations *before* and *after* crossing the line.

Case Manager Approach

Case managers can be the good (traffic) cops, advocates for the best interests of beleaguered employees. Though they are not psychological counselors, case managers can orchestrate setting up a variety of counseling resources and can communicate and coordinate with all relevant parties.

A case manager approach makes the process of getting help more human as compared to being handled by a cold bureaucratic machine. Employees will think: *"At least there's one good, decent person I can trust who will watch over my progress from start to finish."*

Case managers can carefully communicate with the home agency and its internal components, such as security and CI. Initial contact with the case manager must be made simple, clear, and easy.

Security Concerns

Concealing the identities of counselors and employees from certain interested parties who have potential to cause trouble will be important. That includes our own security investigators who will initially need to be kept at arm's length. Otherwise, employees will get spooked, which will wreck their trust in the process. Sticking to such careful guidelines will preserve the new prevention program's good corridor reputation. Losing a good corridor reputation risks wrecking the whole program.

FIE agents would also be threats. They would love to know who is in severe distress because, of course, these are the employees who would be their best targets to recruit.

MAKING THE NEW PREVENTION PROGRAM WORK

■ TARGETING THE CORRECT AUDIENCE

Who are the correct targets? To make the new prevention program work, it is essential to know with whom you are dealing. Potential insider threat actors are described in my *White Paper, Part One: True Psychology of the Insider Spy.*

Potential insider threat actors are feeling desperate. They process their overwhelming life situations from distorted perspectives, mirroring the mindsets of patients with clinical anxiety and depression. They are not thinking like their usual selves. They are operating with skewed logic and a dark worldview, pessimistic and hopeless. Their sense of time has collapsed into a constant terrible Now, with no memory of a better past or any anticipation of a better future. Their extreme emotional states may include:

- Depression
- Demoralization
- Broken pride
- Feeling like a failure
- Desperation
- Agitation
- Scared
- Panicked
- Struggling
- Drowning
- Exhausted

- Poor judgment
- Inability to focus
- Angry and aggressive in all directions

After the crisis passes, they will not believe they were temporarily so totally captured by such twisted emotions and logic. As they get restored back to their usual competent selves, they will dramatically shift to more positive perspectives.

■ COMMUNICATING THE RIGHT WAY WITH THE TARGET AUDIENCE

Adopt the Proper Tone
Speak to their desperation, inner hurt, and pain; not to their outward prickly defenses. See the lessons from the previous discussion of handling hostage takers.

Engage by Making Offers Instead of Threats:

- Lifelines with reassurances
- Quick, immediate help
- Respectful tones that preserve pride
- No threats

- Safe
- Framed as the *manly* thing to do
- Emphasize *hope*

Off-ramp exit options would be proposed as the employee's choice to make, freely, voluntarily, and only when ready. Offering choices is always preferable. Even children prefer choices. Choices work better than forcing demands, which just raises resistance. Remember the old saying: "You can catch more flies with honey than with vinegar."

■ PACKAGING OFFERS
Offers must be sensible and attractive. Offers must address prospects in respectful terms, packaged in ways that will restore the employee's sensitive bruised ego. Offers must preserve the employee's pride and dignity. There would be no room for authoritarian, scolding, threatening, or coercive messages. Done this way, offers restore hope to an employee on the ropes, overwhelmed and impaired by compromised thinking and logic.

NEW PREVENTION PROGRAM SHOULD BE ROLLED OUT IN PHASES

■ PHASE ONE: REDEFINING THE MEANING OF SPYING
Redefining the meaning of spying would be a critical first step that sets the stage for changing basic assumptions about spies and insider threat actors.

For example, current basic assumptions and theories about insider spies are that they are simply bad people, criminals, evil schemers, and traitors to their bones. Certain personality characteristics have been attributed to insider spies who were studied, such as *narcissistic, grandiose, antisocial,* etc.[15] When examined more closely, these diagnostic terms can be better understood as *defensive* in nature. They serve to cover up to the world, and more so, to themselves, the deeper core problem of insider spies: *An intolerable sense of personal failure, as privately defined by that person.*

These negative characterizations, while not wrong, are superficial. They do not help much in identifying potential or active insider threat actors since they are found so frequently in all populations, especially in high-performance, driven professionals. They are not precise enough to warrant investigating the many employees who are wired this way. Can you picture saying to an employee: *"We think you are arrogant, so we have to take away your clearance."*

These pejorative terms, though they sound diagnostically significant, do not amount to much more than after-the-fact name-calling. To discern the core psychology from which these tendencies originate, delving deeper is important. Going beyond characterizing spies as just being evil criminals is necessary.

Paradoxically, in our country, being bad can be an attractive identity and pose. Spies may be oddly proud of being BAD. Working to change the real meaning of spying from being BAD to being SAD becomes a useful goal.

Simply put, spies are unhappy people who have failed in their lives.

They are not so much evil, malicious criminals as hurt, injured, fragile, failing people. They see themselves as Losers and Failures. The *redefined meaning of spying* is solidly based on key *NOIR White Paper* ideas. These ideas should be referenced because they go a long way towards explaining what is behind the drastically bad decision to cross the line.

More on Redefining What Spying Really Means

Crossing the line is no longer to be defined as just being a criminal, vengeful, evil act of a defiant outlaw (although it is all these things). Because there is a dark attraction in our country to being labeled in these negative terms, why go along with something that just adds gasoline to the fire? There is truth to the old saying: "People would rather be hated than ignored." Ignored in this case means being regarded as small and insignificant, intolerable for any man's sense of pride.

The decision to spy must be transformed in the minds of the general public, and especially within the minds of the IC workforce, into something rather different:

Crossing the line is more a desperate and profoundly sad act that reveals evidence of a fellow human being's ultimate failure. It reveals that a broken coworker became a pathetic human train wreck, whose last-ditch effort to feel better about himself was to cross the line.

Can a Commonly Held Assumptions Be Changed? Yes, If Done Right

CASE EXAMPLE:
Trashed Texas Highways Get Cleaned Up

When citizens of Texas had enough of their littered and trashed highways, they brainstormed ways to get them cleaned up. They created a program with the catchy slogan: "Don't mess with Texas."[16]

This slogan appealed not only to famous Texas pride but also to individual masculine pride and ego. No Texas dude ever wants to be messed with. That would be an intolerable insult. With the new catchy slogan, individual male attitudes about pride were extended and attached to the entire sovereign state of Texas. Now, not trashing Texas highways became not just a matter of individual pride but also of collective pride, joining something that always had personal meaning to a *larger purpose*. Messing up Texas highways was now conflated with messing with each and every Texan's personal reputation. Don't ever think about getting away with that!

To disseminate the new message took a concerted program costing time, energy and money. But when the desired attitude took hold, Texas highways got clean.

Redefining the real meaning of spying within the general population and the IC workforce will take about two years of concerted effort.

How *Redefining the Meaning of Spying* Helps Change Inner Calculations

Redefining the meaning of crossing the line, from *bad* to *sad*, builds a self-limiting mental barrier that will work internally on prospective spies, forcing them to reconsider their impending rash decisions. For the sake of their residual pride, they will redouble their efforts to work out different, saner solutions.

Implanting the new meaning of insider spying inside the minds of employees on the brink to "Not so much bad as sad," will build *internal resistance* to allowing any further slide down the slippery slope. What remains of their personal pride will now come to the rescue: "I'm *not* a loser/failure. I *can* find another way to beat this!"

Any employee contemplating crossing the line will be preconditioned to know what crossing the line will mean, not just to themselves, but to everyone else: That they have *utterly failed as a person*, a shameful reputation to have to live with.

They will have to anticipate that, if they do cross the line and do get caught, the public will eventually hear their story of betrayal. The public will share an instant understanding of what it really means. Instead of caught spies being on the receiving end of mere anger, they will be on the receiving end of *pity*.

No one wants to feel pitied.

The redefinition, from *bad* to *sad*, will be coupled with the companion message that when you know you need help, it is the manly thing to reach for it.

Again, the words of the song *"Lean on Me"*[14] capture the right tone to be communicated.

■ *PHASE TWO: PROVING THE REDEFINED MEANING OF SPYING*

You cannot make a big claim without providing proof. Fortunately, the proof is not hard to come by to support the narrative that in the months before deciding to cross the line, most potential insider spies have suffered a severe and *sad* downward spiral in their lives. You do not have to make up the stories. The tragic stories of caught insider spies showing this linkage are already very well known. The stories give support and life to the proposed redefinition.

> When unhappy people lose control of their lives and lose their self-respect is when they start their downward slides, the precise state of mind that makes them candidates for crossing the line and perpetrating insider threat events.

These sad stories just need to be gathered together and presented as examples proving the point, making the case that a fellow human being, under extreme stress conditions, broke under pressure. When unhappy people lose control of their lives and lose their self-respect is when they start their downward slides, the precise state of mind that makes them candidates for crossing the line and perpetrating insider threat events.

There is nothing here to admire. Rather, it is a sad and depressing story when overwhelming life pressures destroy a good intelligence officer.

Spying will get recast as *equivalent to the worst personal humiliations.* Spying would get redefined as the adult equivalent of the worst humiliation that can occur to a kindergarten kid: Making in your pants. There is no honor or anything good to say about it. It is embarrassing, all too obvious (it stinks), and worst of all, shows everyone else that you are still just a baby!

Does it matter that this redefinition fully explains every single case? No.

Consider the Power of Memes

Memes are ideas or notions that propagate through populations somewhat like biological genes, though mainly by word of mouth, or these days, through social media. If an idea or meme sticks, it develops a life of its own and spreads virally. If most people come to believe the explanation makes sense, it will become the shared, accepted truth.

The mere repetition of memes makes them gain acceptance if there are enough supporting proofs to back them up. Given enough time, the redefined meaning of spying will change to:

> *Some unfortunate coworker couldn't handle his life stresses and got broken by the pressure. That is why he crossed the line.*
>
> *Spying is the ultimate proof that he was destroyed, reduced to be a complete loser, a total failure.*
>
> *What a pity he broke. How sad and disappointing.*

■ *PHASE THREE: GETTING THE MESSAGES OUT*

Messages must be proactively publicized and implanted into the minds of the general public and the IC workforce by using techniques from the worlds of marketing, advertising, and promotion. No need here to describe the advanced publicity methods practiced in our country for decades.

Focus groups could come up with the best language, words, and phrases to use for capturing attention and being well received. Messages must be coupled with appeals to residual pride and ego.

For example: *"If you really put your mind to it, you can find other ways to solve your worst life crisis. Better ways. More mature and adult ways. You can dig your way out of your hole. Don't dig the hole any deeper!"*

Outreach to the General Public

Limiting this campaign to just the IC workforce is not enough by itself. The redefinition must be shared throughout the entire culture of our nation to achieve the beneficial effect of changing internal calculations about what it means to cross the line. Everyone on the edge of crossing the line will have to calculate how their decision will later play inside the minds of fellow employees, friends, family, and the general public.

NEW SECURITY TRAINING FOR THE IC WORKFORCE

Semi-Annual Computerized Training

The *Core Psychology of the Insider Spy* and the *Ten Life Stages of the Insider Spy* should be taught, as well as the redefinition of what spying (or becoming an insider threat actor) really means, as described above.

The redefined meaning of spying must be proven with true sad life stories as evidence. Themes to be explored will include: What were the life pressures that set up troubled employees to get into their difficulties, what were the backgrounds that sensitized them, how and why did they break under the pressure? There would be dramatized portrayals of typical crisis situations that are paired with portrayals of alternative scenarios showing how to better handle similar life stresses.

New helping resources will be described

The first message to be conveyed is that things are different from the way they used to be. In the past, helping resources may have been regarded as not so safe or trustworthy, maybe even too dangerous to try. Employees used to avoid seeking help for fear it could make things even worse. But the situation is better now. IC leadership came to understand the deficiencies and took decisive steps to remedy them. There is now a new prevention program in place, which includes an external EAP, outside every employee's home agency, for those who will feel safer and more comfortable with such a resource.

Examples of life situations that can be helped would be listed. Workarounds would be described as well as the range of resources that are now available.

The new two-tier structure of EAPs would be explained

- The First Tier: Home agency internal EAPs
- The Second Tier: The external EAP

Resources for *after* crossing the line, such as NOIR (should it be stood up), would also be described.

Live Events

- Presentations, lectures, movies
- Panels of actual spies who were caught

Insider spies, whether still incarcerated or now released, would tell their stories in their own words. This event would have powerful impact since the people telling their stories would be former IC employees. Their stories would be told candidly, pulling no punches, recounting their unhappy experiences with the sadder-but-wiser lessons they learned. This would resemble panels of impaired MDs who have told their stories to fellow physicians, an enormously powerful experience for such audiences.

MESSAGING

Messaging must be to the entire IC workforce

Of course, that is mostly preaching to the choir because nearly the entire IC workforce is solidly loyal, patriotic and would never think of crossing the line.

True targets are those who are currently severely stressed and vulnerable

It is especially necessary to speak to them. If they are not moved by this outreach, there is no chance of effective prevention. Messaging must reach those who are "on the ledge," already deeply mired in desperate situations. Words, phrases, and language must be used that can still reach and move them. Messages must offer empathy and rays of hope, and resources that are safe, make sense, and that would be regarded as credible rescue options.

Messages must go under the radar by communicating caring concern

The tone of messaging can no longer be the usual messages consisting of dire warnings not to cross the line, that threaten severe punishments, or that admonish with negative, scolding tones. Messages communicated in a "military voice" will be reacted to with anger or will just be ignored.

Messages must go under their defensive radar and speak to their underlying *intolerable sense of personal failure*. The revised tones must communicate concern and sorrow for coworkers and teammates who are no longer able to manage their lives and who are feeling overwhelmed, desperate, cornered, drowning.

The new tones would show that the IC understands that they are feeling desperate, hopeless, exhausted and out of ideas of how to steer their lives and survive.

By accurately identifying how they are feeling and communicating that understanding in language and words that penetrate through their mental fog and confusion, the new caring and persuasive messages will not get deflected so easily and will penetrate false defensives. Employees "on the ledge" will be thrown off balance *in a good way* by these caring messages. They will be forced to face themselves without the protection of their chosen armor.

Given the psychological truth of what is going on, aren't these new messages more on target and appealing?

If a sailor falls overboard, you don't lecture him from the rail about why he should have taken more swimming lessons. You throw him a lifeline!

Not: *"We watch everything you do and if you cross the line, we'll catch you, you slime!"*

LOCATE SECOND-TIER PREVENTION RESOURCES UNDER THE ODNI

Despite initial misgivings about the Office of the Director of National Intelligence (ODNI), its mission has been to make the entire IC work more effectively. Located within the ODNI, the external to the home agency EAP prevention function would provide a valuable resource that could be made available across all sixteen IC agencies. As explained, it is important for the perception of safety to have an external, second-tier resource that operates outside of the other sixteen IC agencies, thus able to act as a third party with its many advantages.

■ *BEST PRACTICES*

For the sake of improving the prevention function, refining it would be better accomplished within one central, expert setting. Otherwise, best practice refinements may get lost inside the stovepipes of the sixteen separate IC agencies. Learning how to set up helping resources will be based on best practices borrowed from existing successful counseling systems, combined with IC tradecraft knowledge.

ODNI-located resources can house the two key capabilities that should *not* be housed in the individual agencies:

- The second-tier external EAP, the EAP "at a higher level"
- NOIR

Detection must still be conducted by security and CI within each IC agency

Detection is still a critical function that must be performed by each agency's security and CI components. They are familiar with the details and culture of their respective agencies.

Could someone abuse the proposed prevention system? Not to worry.

What about concern that some scheming employees might abuse and exploit the new prevention system? Maybe they just want to escape their job and take the easy way out?

Please don't throw me into that briar patch!

This should not be regarded as abuse. This should be thought of as a gift from God.

If someone reaches out to the second-tier level of help as their plan to "abuse" or "exploit" the system, so what? Aren't these the very employees that you would desperately want to be removed from access to classified materials? If they want out that badly, don't you also want them out even more? Isn't that far better than the alternative: a sudden deluge of classified materials released to our adversaries or to the public?

The price to exit such types will be tiny compared to the cost of the damages they might otherwise inflict. Whatever the costs, it is still cheaper to handle it this way. Remember the genie question posed earlier. There is no point being "penny wise, pound-foolish."

Some may be genuinely difficult people

Still, a soft-glove approach should be employed. It is important for the IC to keep eyes on the prize: What is it that nets out best for the IC? What meets the crucial goal of more successfully preventing insider threat events?

■ EMPLOYEES TEMPORARILY IMMUNE TO PREVENTION MESSAGES

Whistleblowers

Early in the game, they may see themselves as strictly motivated by high-minded, "noble" intentions. Their rationalizations are still too attractive to them. That can change.

THE BRIAR PATCH

The "briar patch" noted above harkens back to the proverbial stories of Uncle Remus, an African-American version of Aesop's Fables, compiled by Joel Chandler Harris, that illustrate human nature and foibles.

Brer Fox captures Brer Rabbit. This could be the end for Brer Rabbit, but Brer Rabbit starts moaning, groaning, and crying. He begs Brer Fox to do anything he wants, tear him limb from limb, but *"please, please, don't throw me into that briar patch!"*

Brer Fox cannot help but decide that if throwing Brer Rabbit into the briar patch would inflict the very worst on that rabbit, that's exactly what he will do! Of course, Brer Rabbit is steps ahead of Brer Fox. He knows the briar patch is impossible for the fox to navigate, whereas as a rabbit, he can get along fine inside the briars, and will be able to escape to live another day.

No one in the IC would want to have a risky person "get away" with the easy outs proposed by the off-ramp exits I have proposed. But that misses the IC's highest goal regarding insider threat: Stop it cold, get them out if necessary, and do so at whatever cost! It is infinitely cheaper to manage potential enormous losses of classified information that way as compared to all the alternatives.

Employees with ethnic, ideological, or religious motives

In the early stages of their recruitment, clever appeals and arguments invoking such tribal loyalties may still be too convincing to them. Initial compelling motivations can change over time since such rationales often weaken over time.

Psychopathic and antisocial types

These personality types are unlikely to be moved by appeals to seek help. However, all is not lost. For strictly selfish reasons, when they calculate it is advantageous for them, they may decide to reach for help anyhow. Is that a problem? Why? They would have to *voluntarily self-identify* and now become visible. This alone will cause them to have to cease their harmful activities. The IC would still be in better shape because now, having even partial knowledge of their identities, the situation would be much better than having no knowledge of them. This affords the IC a great advantage compared to merely hoping that someday, perhaps many years from now, detection will luck out and disclose them.

Not yet ready

Employees who are just not yet ready because they are still too preoccupied with their internal mental struggles to consider alternatives. Exit options will have to wait a while longer until changing life circumstances will increase their readiness.

NO CLAIM THIS NEW PREVENTION PROGRAM IS A PERFECT SOLUTION

Imperfect is good enough. As they say: "The perfect is the enemy of the good." No program will ever be perfect and work for all insider threat actors. Less than perfect outcomes are predictable, but that is better than a multitude of really terrible outcomes. The proposed new prevention program is guided by the notion: *Problems can be solved, messes must be managed.*

The primary goal is to significantly reduce the prevalence of insider threat events.

NOIR can be the backstop for those who were not persuaded by the new prevention program and still choose to cross the line. NOIR is for those who later experience an awakening and voluntarily decide to quit their treasonous activities. If the new prevention program advocated here does not capture insider threat actors *before* they choose to cross the line, there is still the chance to capture them *after* they have crossed the line – but only if NOIR also gets stood up as the companion back-end resource.

LEGAL HURDLES TO BE OVERCOME

Do these three NOIR white papers with their proposed novel and controversial mechanisms assume there will be no conflicts with our existing system of laws related to insider threat and spying?

While I am not an attorney, it does not mean I am completely naïve. Adoption of the NOIR proposals would surely encounter serious conflicts with existing laws, procedures and practices. That is why buy-in from all agencies of the IC, especially the Department of Justice (DOJ), would be necessary. Acceptance by Congress, the White House and the general public would also be necessary. A very hard sell.

That said, roughly the same set of barriers and hurdles existed when the Witness Protection Program (WITSEC) was first proposed decades ago. For WITSEC to gain acceptance from the interested parties mentioned above was initially seen as virtually impossible. Fortunately, WITSEC was backed strongly by then Attorney General, Robert Kennedy, and of course, by his brother, President John F. Kennedy. Both were determined to bring down the American Mafia. They decided this could only be accomplished by creating a safe exit mechanism for Mafia gangsters, who could then tell their incriminating tales, though still at real risk to their lives. It worked.

Hard decisions were made at the highest levels to subordinate national revulsion at giving a pass to criminals and murderers in exchange for the strategic advantage of ridding our country of an even greater evil, the Mafia. Gerald Shur of the DOJ was the hero attorney who guided WITSEC through all the legal barriers, at some personal risk of his own. WITSEC continues to operate effectively today, managed by the United States Marshals Service.

As with WITSEC, overcoming the legal hurdles that will permit NOIR proposals to successfully get adopted will take a lot of hard work. Similarly, it will be worth it.

NOIR concepts were partly inspired by and echo the story of WITSEC, adjusted for utility within the IC. Critical benefits of admittedly controversial programs sometimes can be sufficiently advantageous to justify the difficult accommodations that would be required to give them life. Especially so when the stakes are so important – our national survival. With the aim of much improved management of insider threat, there is a rationale to change existing laws when the stakes are existential. Quoting Justice Robert H. Jackson: "The Constitution is not a suicide pact."[17]

SECTION H

CONCLUSIONS

DETECTION IS NECESSARY BUT NOT SUFFICIENT

Within the IC, most thinking and resources have gone into detection even though exclusive reliance on detection has not proven to work that well. Of course, detection is clearly absolutely necessary and works up to a point. Unfortunately, when a determined insider decides to defeat detection measures, they succeed all too frequently. Relying exclusively on detection is insufficient. We need more tools in our toolkit.

MISSING LINKS: TWO OFF-RAMP EXITS

Two important links are missing for creating a *full spectrum solution* for better management of insider threat: Off-ramp exits for *before* and off-ramp exits for *after* someone crosses the line.

TO MOVE "LEFT OF BOOM," A FULL SPECTRUM SOLUTION IS NEEDED

Solutions to be added are based on a better understanding of the psychology of insider threat actors. The three most important strategies that are advocated in this paper:

1. **Elevating IMIT approaches to managing insider threat**, as opposed to almost exclusive reliance on EMIT approaches

2. **Redefining the meaning of spying** to build self-imposed inner resistance in the minds of troubled employees, to help prevent any further inclination to cross the line. Residual pride will come to the rescue.

3. **Improving existing EAPs and adding novel EAP resources** will provide exit solutions that are safer for troubled employees to access. These enhanced helping resources will work to restore what troubled employees are sorely lacking: *Hope.*

COMBINING FRONT AND BACK-END SOLUTIONS

Building off-ramp exit solutions for before and for after someone crosses the line would add the two most glaring missing links that are necessary to establish a *full spectrum solution* for effectively managing insider threat.

If it is not possible to head off insider threat actors *before* they cross the line, then the next best thing is to stop them *after* they cross the line, and the sooner, the better (NOIR). Simultaneously standing up both proposed off-ramp exit solutions would be more efficient, effective and practical.

FINAL MESSAGE

- We all share a common goal – protect our nation's security from insider spies and insider threats

- We have a number of tools in our tool kit: prevention, detection, deterrence through prosecution, etc.

- We have challenges and opportunities in all of these areas

- None of these tools, alone or in combination, is a silver bullet

- Detection using big data analytics, ML and AI may become revolutionary but are not problem-free

- NOIR proposals add more tools to our toolkit: exit ramps for before or after someone crosses the line

- Adding the new resources proposed in my three NOIR papers is not a choice to be made in opposition to detection – they are complementary to detection

Will the IC take up the challenge of managing its insider threat risk by going beyond mainly relying on detection? Will the IC strengthen its insider threat posture by adopting the new prevention strategies proposed in this paper?

There is hope. Churchill supposedly said: "Americans can always be counted to do the right thing... after they've tried all the other possibilities."

ENDNOTES

[1] Sun Tzu, James Trapp (trans.), "Chapter VII: Maneuvers Against the Enemy" in *The Art of War*, (New York: Chartwell Books, 2016): 47.

[2] *NOIR White Papers*: The first paper, entitled "True Psychology of the Insider Spy," was first published in the *The Intelligencer* 18 (1) Fall/Winter 2010 47-54. *The Intelligencer* is the official journal of the Association of Former Intelligence Officers (AFIO). The paper was republished as a special attachment to *The Intelligencer*, as Part One of a two-part White Paper, entitled "NOIR, A White Paper." Part Two was entitled, "Proposing a New Policy For Improving National Security By Fixing the Problem of Insider Spies." To access all three NOIR White Papers, which are available online as PDFs, please refer to our website: NOIR4USA.org.

[3] Martin Handford. First published in London as *Where's Wally?* (London: Walker Books, 1987). There have been numerous follow-on volumes.

[4] German Democratic Republic (GDR) Ministry for State Security (*Ministerium für Staatssicherheit*, MfS, Stasi) was the East German state security service, with both internal and external functions. In its internal functions, it is a classic example of a secret police force controlling a national population.

[5] See details of the Behavioral Stairway Model at the Viaconflict Website, 26 October 2014: https://viaconflict.wordpress.com/2014/10/26/the-behavioral-change-stairway-model/

[6] An excellent and thorough treatment of the development of these softer and more effective interrogation methods can be found in "The long read: The scientists persuading terrorists to spill their secrets," London *Guardian*, October 13, 2017: https://www.theguardian.com/news/2017/oct/13/the-scientists-persuading-terrorists-to-spill-their-secrets.

[7] As an example of the mounting concern, consider the following title of an industry publication with the wake-up call: "In 2017, The Insider Threat Epidemic Begins" by James Scott and Drew Spaniel (February 2017). http://icitech.org/wp-content/uploads/2017/02/ICIT-Brief-In-2017-The-Insider-Threat-Epidemic-Begins.pdf.

[8] Mike Rogers, former chairman of the House Special Select Committee on Intelligence, is quoted to this effect in Julien Hattem, "Former Intelligence chairman: More spies than ever," *The Hill*, 30 March 2016: http://thehill.com/policy/national-security/274704-former-intel-chairman-more-foreign-spies-in-us-than-ever-before.

[9] John R. Schindler addresses this issue in "Our National Security's Millennial Problem," *The Observer*, 14 October 2017: http://observer.com/2017/10/snowden-winner-manning-nsa-millennial-problem/.

[10] Alden Munson wrote a biting account of his experiences in "Why Can't We Get Acquisitions Right?" in *STEPS: Science, Technology, and Engineering Policy Studies*, October 2017. He describes the forces that work against sanity in how government sets about acquiring new systems as "the Conspiracy of Hope." http://www.potomacinstitute.org/featured-news/1800-why-can-t-we-get-acquisitions-right-by-alden-munson

[11] Will Knight, "The Dark Secret at the Heart of AI," *MIT Technology Review*, 11 April 2017: https://www.technologyreview.com/s/604087/the-dark-secret-at-the-heart-of-ai/

[12] Will Knight, "Biased Algorithms Are Everywhere, and No One Seems to Care," *MIT Technology Review*, 12 July 2017: https://www.technologyreview.com/s/608248/biased-algorithms-are-everywhere-and-no-one-seems-to-care/.

[13] Judge Webster addressed this concern in private conversation with me.

[14] *Lean on Me* is a 1972 song that says it all. For a great performance, listen to the rendition recorded in 2009 by the country group Nothin' Fancy. See: https://www.youtube.com/watch?v=ZKzT1yrrlDc. Also see song lyrics below.

[15] These psychological and psychiatric terms show up in the IC's most ambitious attempts at studying insider threat: the 1990 Project *Slammer* and the Defense Department Defense Personnel and Security Research Center (PERSEREC) studies.

[16] "Don't mess with Texas" website, www.dontmesswithtexas.org.

[17] https://en.wikipedia.org/wiki/The_Constitution_is_not_a_suicide_pact.

Lean on Me

Written by Bill Withers • Copyright © Universal Music Publishing Group

Sometimes in our lives we all have pain
We all have sorrow
But if we are wise
We know that there's always tomorrow

Lean on me, when you're not strong
And I'll be your friend
I'll help you carry on
For it won't be long
'Til I'm gonna need
Somebody to lean on

Please swallow your pride
If I have faith you need to borrow
For no one can fill those of your needs
That you won't let show

You just call on me brother, when you need a hand
We all need somebody to lean on
I just might have a problem that you'll understand
We all need somebody to lean on

Lean on me, when you're not strong
And I'll be your friend
I'll help you carry on
For it won't be long
'Til I'm gonna need
Somebody to lean on

You just call on me brother, when you need a hand
We all need somebody to lean on
I just might have a problem that you'll understand
We all need somebody to lean on

If there is a load you have to bear
That you can't carry
I'm right up the road
I'll share your load

If you just call me (call me)
If you need a friend (call me) call me uh huh(call me)
if you need a friend (call me)
If you ever need a friend (call me)
Call me (call me) call me (call me) call me
(Call me) call me (call me) if you need a friend
(Call me) call me (call me) call me (call me) call me
(call me) call me (call me)

ABOUT THE AUTHOR
David L. Charney, MD

Dr. Charney is the Founder and Medical Director of Roundhouse Square Counseling Center, in Alexandria, Virginia. He specializes in Anxiety and Mood Disorders, Couples and Family Therapy, as well as Attention Deficit Disorder in adults.

In addition to his usual practice, he has also treated personnel from within the Intelligence Community. As a result of unusual circumstances, he had the opportunity to join the defense team of his first spy case, Earl Pitts. Subsequently, Plato Cacheris, the attorney of Robert Hanssen, invited Dr. Charney to join his defense team, which added a further dimension to his experience. With the addition of his third spy case, Brian Regan, Dr. Charney further deepened his knowledge of the psychological nuances of captured spies.

As a member of their defense teams, Dr. Charney was perceived by these insider spies as an understanding and supportive figure, which lowered their defensive mindsets, and provided a truer picture of their inner lives. Many common assumptions of spy motivation were brought into question by Dr. Charney's work.

Dr. Charney elaborated his findings in Part One of his White Paper, entitled *True Psychology of the Insider Spy*. Part Two of his White Paper, entitled *NOIR*, lays out Dr. Charney's innovative and perhaps controversial recommendations for making use of what he learned to better manage the problem of insider spies. To educate and promote these concepts and ideas, he founded NOIR for USA, a non-profit organization. Its website is: NOIR4USA.org.

READ MORE ON
www.NOIR4USA.ORG

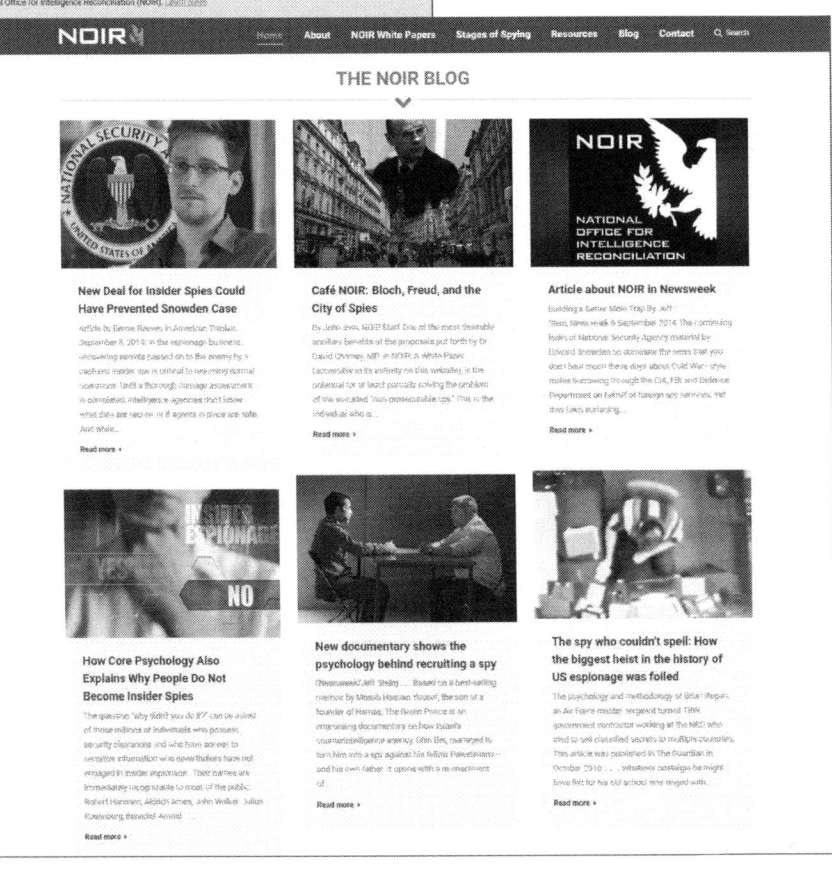

Dr. David Charney is available for interviews and briefings about the NOIR concept. We're also interested in knowing what you think about NOIR and welcome your feedback and thoughts.

NOIR for USA
c/o David L. Charney, MD
1501 Duke Street, Suite 100
Alexandria, VA 22314
703-836-7130
contact@noir4usa.org

NOIR

NATIONAL
OFFICE FOR
INTELLIGENCE
RECONCILIATION

Printed in Great Britain
by Amazon